HOW THE OTHER HALF LIVED

Ludlow's working classes 1850–1960

DEREK BEATTIE

MERLIN UNWIN BOOKS

First published in the UK by Merlin Unwin Books Ltd, 2016
Text © Derek Beattie 2016
All rights reserved, including the right to reproduce this book or portions thereof in any form or by any means, electronic or mechanical, including photocopying, recording, or by any information storage and retrieval system, without permission in writing from the publisher:

>Merlin Unwin Books Ltd
>Palmers House
>7 Corve Street
>Ludlow
>Shropshire SY8 1DB
>U.K.
>www.merlinunwin.co.uk

The author asserts his moral right to be identified with this work.
ISBN 978-1-910723-34-0
Typeset in 12 point Bembo by Merlin Unwin Books
Printed in the UK by Jellyfish Print Solutions

This book is dedicated to:

My maternal grandmother who was illegitimate and brought up in a small Norfolk fishing village.

My maternal grandfather who was illegitimate and whose illiterate mother gave birth while serving a sentence in Her Majesty's Prison Cheetham Hill, Manchester (Strangeways).

My paternal grandmother who was the daughter of a village blacksmith in Aberdeenshire.

My paternal grandfather whose widowed mother died in the Aberdeen Poorhouse.

>They all knew how the other half lived.

Contents

1 The Background to Working Class Ludlow 1
2 Sewerage, Drains, Privies and Water Closets 23
3 Water and its Domestic Uses 41
4 Housing Conditions 64
5 Health and Health Care 85
6 Life on the Edge of Poverty 116
7 The Arrival of the Council House 148
Footnotes 171
Interviewees 177
Index 181
Acknowledgements 185

iv   *How the Other Half Lived*

These 1885 maps of Ludlow show the concentration of back-building that resulted in the many Yards and Courts that hid behind the town's street-scape (see Chapter 1).

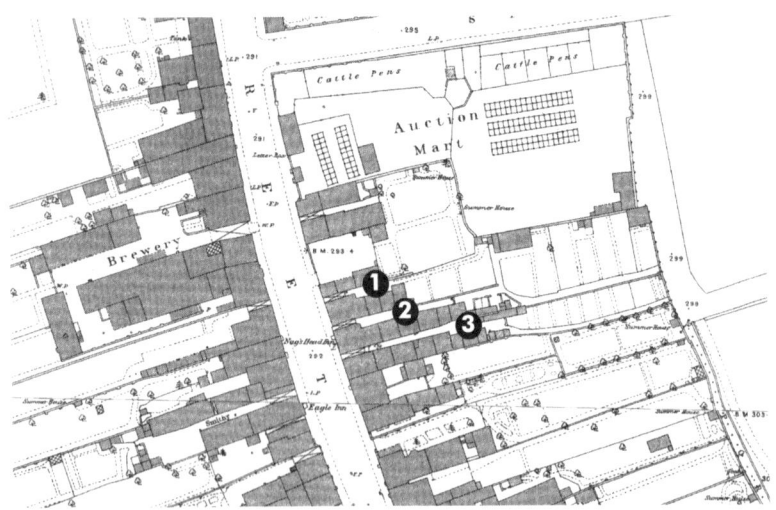

1. Drew's Court   2. Nag's Head Yard   3. Hammond's Yard

1. King's Arms Yard   2. Pardoe's Yard (?)   3. Noakes' Yard   4. Dean's Yard
5. Weaver's Yard

CHAPTER ONE

The Background to Working Class Ludlow

The history of the castle, the parish church and the main buildings and institutions of Ludlow has been described in a number of publications [as has the history of many of the social, economic and political hierarchies of the town]. However, the bulk of the population of Ludlow over the centuries has largely been ignored except, perhaps, as the anonymous workers who helped make the profits on which their employers lived or who provided the services that their 'betters' required. This book attempts to redress this for the period 1850-1960. An attempt is made to shine a light on the housing and living conditions of the majority of the populace of Ludlow who were often forced to dwell in cramped, overcrowded, dark and damp properties with few facilities. As a result life was hard, especially for the wives and mothers who, on a limited budget, had to keep the house tidy, the family in clean clothes and ensure that food was always on the table. And all this often had to be done against a backdrop of ill health.

Ludlow's economic boom years were in the 18th and early 19th centuries when glove making became the staple industry of the town. By 1815 there were twelve glove-makers listed employing 735 people many of whom were women and children. There were a few workshops, mainly situated behind

DINHAM BACK-BUILDING
Back-building occurred in virtually every nook and cranny in the centre of Ludlow. In 1960 this row of working class cottages, entered by a narrow, brick-paved alleyway between numbers 2 and 7 Dinham, could still be seen. They have now either been demolished or incorporated into the properties that face the street.
(Courtesy of Stanton Stephens)

the houses of the glove masters where the leather was cut. The pieces were then taken to the outworkers in their homes to be stitched into gloves. The shape of the working class areas of the town was now fashioned when an expansion of poor quality, cheap building, much of it speculative, took place in order to house the expanding number of these outworkers.

This new housing tended to be built on the gardens behind the properties that faced the various streets. This in turn meant that in areas in the centre of town all available space was filled. To gain access to these buildings, as well as using paths down the sides of properties, what often happened was that a property facing a street had an alleyway built through it, often dividing it into two smaller houses. In order to have as many houses as possible on a piece of land, some of these buildings were built attached to the back of the original houses, cutting off all light and access from behind and, in effect, turning them into back-to-back dwellings. In order to build the maximum amount of properties on a limited space, many of the new cottages were also very small: either just one

The Background to Working Class Ludlow

room up and one room down or one room down and two up.

The result of this type of building can perhaps be better understood by looking at individual streets. On the east side of Corve Street could be found four courts of cottages. These would be entered by narrow alleyways and the houses may have faced a small open space in which could be found a communal privy or privies and a wash-house. Alternatively, such outbuildings could have been erected at the end of a row of properties. Later, an outside communal water tap would have been added. Travelling down Corve Street the first court was met just before the Nag's Head public house. This was officially known as Number 1 Court but known locally as Hammond's Court after Herbert Hammond, a grocer who lived at No. 132. As will be seen, in most official records such as the ten-yearly census, these courts were often

DREW'S COURT
This is Drew's Court just before WWI. It was entered by the side of 119, Corve Street that in 1881 was the home of Mary Drew, a dressmaker. This is typical of the many yards and courts built behind the respectable facades of Ludlow's main thoroughfares. The poor, original quality of the buildings can be discerned in the crumbling and twisted nature of the brickwork and the ill-fitting windows. Though they had no garden space residents made do with what they had and two homemade pigeon coops can be seen attached to the wall opposite their doors. These properties now lie underneath Tesco.
(Courtesy of Lottie James)

just recognised numerically. However, local people tended to name them after the builder or main landlord or even a tenant, sometimes notorious in reputation, who happened to live there. Because of this, the names of some yards or courts changed over time as the properties changed hands or as a new generation came into being.

Next in Corve Street came No. 2 Court known as the Nag's Head Yard, followed by No. 3 Court or Drew's Yard named after Mary Drew, a dressmaker who lived at its entrance. Finally came No. 4 Court or the Green Dragon Yard. This last yard was, in fact, one of the earliest to be built with three cottages being constructed, probably in 1772, by the innkeeper.[1] A further three cottages were later added. This was a pattern seen all over Ludlow with the number of properties in the yards and courts being added to as and when someone could borrow the monies to invest in a fresh round of building. As will be seen, this meant that the cottages in many of these yards and courts, especially after a few decades

KING'S ARMS YARD

This is the King's Arms Yard in 1916. Situated behind the King's Arms public house on the Bull Ring (now the Edinburgh Woollen Mill) it was entered by alleyways off both the Bull Ring and Tower Street. John Fury, who had a barbershop on Tower Street, was an ex-South African War veteran who is almost certainly dressed up as part of a money-raising event for soldiers at the front. He lived in the property on the left.

(Courtesy of Shropshire Museum Service)

had passed, had a number of different landlords some of whom did not even live locally. In times to come this would make enforcement of improvements by the authorities more difficult to achieve. On the West side of Lower Corve Street four more courts could be found. No. 7 Court was built by the Trustees of the Independent Chapel that was already there. Unsurprisingly, this soon became known as the Old Chapel Yard. Of the other three courts – Nos. 5, 6 and 8 – they appear to have been known locally at one time or another as Preece's Court, Breakwell's Yard and Pearce's Court.

Upper Galdeford saw the greatest concentration of back-building. Between 1774 and 1843 over seventy properties had been built on land behind those fronting the north-west side. The positions of two are known: Page's Yard (that later became known as the Central Hall Yard) and the Greyhound Yard. In addition, at various times there were Sheldon's Yard, Jones' Yard, Price's Yard and the Tin Yard. On the south-east side could be found Shenton's Yard where eleven cottages were built in stages between 1782-1807. This was later re-named St Stephen's Yard.

A large amount of back-building was also seen in Lower Galdeford, an area that by the early twentieth century was to contain some of the worst housing in the borough. By 1809, on the north side where it meets Upper Galdeford, seven cottages had been built in what became known as the Three Horseshoes Yard. By the end of the nineteenth century a few of the cottages built during this back-building boom were replaced by better quality housing for the workers. Cottages built on what had been the town pound (animal enclosure) were demolished and replaced by new homes known as Pynfold Close. A similar fate awaited the seventeen cottages built between 1791 and 1835 in Warrington's Yard, the new group of properties being named Warrington Gardens. However, on the south side, such homes were not replaced. A few could be found in Tallowfat Yard built behind a candle factory slightly uphill of where the National School would be built. Uphill from there at least nine small courts comprising two, three or four properties could be found.

A number were reached by alleyways built through the ground floor of existing houses dividing them into two smaller properties. Four were known at one time or another as Badger's Yard, Jones' Yard, Martha Cad's Yard and Burnsnell's Yard. The names of the others have been lost except the passage between what is now Nos. 100 and 104 that is named in Police records as Hince's Yard after a Mrs Milborough Hince, a brothel-house keeper who lived there[2]. Finally, just where Lower Galdeford meets Tower Street, could be found six cottages that made up Weaver's Yard situated just outside the town wall: three were built by 1782 and a further three in the first half of the 19th century.

Old Street too had its quota of yards and courts, two of them (No. 2 and 3 Courts) becoming part of the most squalid area of the town by the beginning of the twentieth century. These were Dean's Yard, where building began in 1771 and which contained eighteen properties by the 1840s, and Noakes' Yard. Building here began in 1802 and had fourteen dwellings by 1811. What remained of both yards was finally demolished and replaced by the Clifton Cinema that opened its doors to the public in 1937. Today it is Clifton Court. Just above these yards could be found Pardoe's Yard (No. 1 Court) that comprised five properties. Further down the street two smaller yards also existed: Chapel Yard and Watkin's Yard. The present Old Street below St John's Road and Friars Walk, and thus outside the town walls, was originally known as Holdgate Fee. Here could be found Grieves' Yard just above the Hen and Chickens public house, whilst on the western side could be discovered Davies' Yard and Grey's Yard, each containing up to four cottages.

The Background to Working Class Ludlow

OLD STREET FRONTING NOAKES' YARD
This accident occurred in 1918 on Old Street when a traction engine timber wagon crashed into the wall of the British School. What cannot be seen is what lay behind the houses. Here could still be found one of the most notorious courts and yards in Ludlow: Noakes' Yard or No. 3 Court that contained fourteen cottages. Just a few years earlier Dean's Yard or No. 2 Court could also be found but since 1901 all eighteen of the cottages had been condemned and emptied of tenants.
(Courtesy of Shropshire Museum Service)

Lower Broad Street was yet another area that underwent extensive back-building. One of the earliest examples of such building took place in 1760 when William Corne, a glover, built an alleyway through the ground floor of No. 68 and built a number of cottages to its rear, presumably to house some of his outworkers. Over the remainder of the eighteenth century and through the early nineteenth century a number of such alleyways were made and properties built on the rear of those fronting the street, especially on the western side. On the eastern side, a passage was driven though a property that was then divided and is now known as numbers 9 and 11 (originally 9 and 13). This led to three new properties behind, known as Hartland's Yard. A similar alley by the side of No. 23 led to nine cottages known originally as Sims Yard and later renamed Taylor's Court. On the other side of the street can still be found two terraces of properties reached by passages now called Whitcliffe Terrace and the Vineyard. Similar backfilling also occurred in parts of Mill Street. Here could be found Maund's Yard entered by a passage by the side of No 32. Named after the landlord Francis Maund, a joiner, three cottages were built before 1814 and a further three and a laundry, complete with a tall chimney, probably during the 1820s. Raven Lane, Dinham and even Broad Street, where six cottages could be reached via a passageway between two fronting shops, numbers 60 and 67, also experienced back-building.

In order to squeeze as many properties as possible into a space and to keep building costs down, most provided only cramped living conditions. Many had just one room on the ground floor in which the family lived, ate and washed, whilst

PEG SELLER

Pedlars, carrying their wares from village to village and town to town were a common sight. They became so numerous that in 1871 they were required to purchase a licence in order to ply their trade. Many had a set route so that regular customers could perhaps expect them every three or four months in order that they could restock. This local pedlar is festooned with hand carved wooden clothes pegs that he is selling door to door.

(Courtesy of Shropshire Museum Service)

The Background to Working Class Ludlow

BLACKSMITH, LOWER CORVE STREET

Many local craftsmen lived and worked in their home. These could be tinsmiths, nailers or in this case a blacksmith who had his smithy by the side of his cottage in Lower Corve Street. Family members, even children, would help in the business as they were taught the trade. It was often their job to ensure coal and water was always on hand, to man the bellows or carry out any other small tasks that needed doing.

(Courtesy of Shropshire Museum Service)

all the household chores such as cooking on the fire range, ironing and the drying of clothes and linen were carried out around them. A staircase would go up to either a single bedroom or to two small bedrooms. Some properties had a small scullery at the rear, though for many this was a luxury still to come. By the end of the nineteenth century, as will be seen in the following chapters, toilet facilities were outside and often shared, as they were to remain for many families until well into the twentieth century, whilst an indoor water supply also remained a far off dream for the majority. A description of Pardoe's Yard at the top of Old Street in 1905, given by the Sanitary Inspector, gives a taste of the conditions that many of these courts and yards, hidden behind the main thoroughfares, were in. On his first inspection in April:

'There were five houses in the court ... The (three shared) water closets were in a bad state, the drains were improperly trapped and the paving of the yard was in such a state as to be of a nuisance. There were no rainwater pipes at the rear of the property, two valley troughs discharging

RAILWAY SHUNTING HORSE

By the end of the nineteenth century Ludlow's early industries had either disappeared or were in decline. The glove industry had been eradicated by 1850 whilst by 1900 the growth of national breweries had caused the town's malting industry to all but disappear. One new area of job expansion came with the railways. Since most goods came or went by rail many new jobs were created and ones that were full time rather than casual. As well as the need for porters, signalmen and railway labourers, the goods yard needed men to work the horses, to move the wagons and to pull the delivery carts. Here, in 1923, is one of the goods yard shunting horses with his handler.   (Courtesy of Shropshire Museum Service)

straight into the yard making the walls very damp.'

A few weeks later one of the three lavatories had become completely blocked and unusable. The cumulative result of such conditions was that 'there was a great deal of illness in the yard amongst the children' a situation that, as will be seen in Chapter 5, was not uncommon.[3]

Overcrowding was also a problem and its extent can be seen in the 1911 census. The cottages in the Greyhound Yard, off Upper Galdeford, were all one room down two rooms up. At No.103 William Cox, a railway platelayer, lived with his wife Sarah. They had had thirteen children of whom eight had survived and all still lived at home. This meant that in the two bedrooms slept the mother and father plus eight children: five daughters and three sons aged from six months to sixteen years. During the day all had to live together in the single downstairs room. At 28 Lower Galdeford James Chandler, a builder's labourer, and his wife Anne lived in a similar sized property. They had had eight children and the six that still lived, aged from three to fifteen years, were still at home together with a two year old granddaughter. Her mother was presumably an elder daughter who had died giving birth. This meant that nine shared the two bedrooms. Further down the road at No. 41, again in a similar sized property, lived John Fury, a general labourer, with his wife Susan and their seven surviving children whose ages ranged from nine months to fourteen years together with a three year old 'adopted' girl. At No. 76 Edward and Alice Penny had to sleep in just one bedroom with their five children, aged one to fourteen years, whilst at No. 35 Frederick and Louisa Penny and their six children aged three months to sixteen years also shared just one bedroom. Numerous other examples of large families living in two or three roomed properties can be found in all working class areas of the town. This includes William Nash, a joiner, who lived at the three roomed 43 Lower Broad Street together with his wife Beatrice and his seven children aged between one and thirteen years.

When allied to poverty, a more intimate picture of what life in an overcrowded cottage could be like was seen in a court case heard in 1899. In a one-up, one-down property in St Mary's Lane lived a husband and wife and their five children aged between one and eight. The landing had to be utilised as a bedroom though the bed had no bed linen. In the only bedroom the bed was covered with just two sheets and part of a counterpane. All were said to be verminous.[4]

Crowded conditions were still being experienced in

Ludlow throughout the twentieth century and remained for many in 1960. Margaret McGarrity, who lived in Taylor's Court off Lower Broad Street until 1952, shared one bedroom with her three siblings whilst her parents slept in the other. Joseph Griffiths, who was the youngest of eight children, lived at 42 Old Street until the late 1940s. All ten had to share two bedrooms. Bob Jones was born in 1954 in a one bedroomed cottage at St Stephen's Yard, off Upper Galdeford, and was one of five children whilst he lived there. There was one bed and two cots in the only bedroom. 'Me Dad got an old pram and took the wheels off it and made it into a rocking cot for one of us.'

As for Bob, as a baby, he slept on the landing in a pulled out bottom drawer of a chest of drawers. Joe Griffiths

LUDLOW WORKHOUSE

Opened in 1839 for the relief of the poor of Ludlow and the surrounding villages, Ludlow Union Workhouse was built to house 250 paupers. Its inmates mainly consisted of widows, abandoned wives, unmarried mothers, orphans, the mentally ill and the elderly. In addition, vagrants and itinerant workers who could not afford a bed for the night were given board. By 1905, when this photograph was taken, such men had to break 5 cwt. of dhustone in exchange for supper, bed and breakfast.

(Courtesy of Shropshire Museum Service)

lived with his parents, one brother and five sisters, in Central Hall Yard off Upper Galdeford. They had two bedrooms. His parents had one, the two boys the other, whilst the five sisters slept in the attic space. Further down the yard, Angie Clare, Alice Pound, their two sisters and parents slept in a one bedroomed cottage until they moved to the Dodmore Estate in 1959. For a while, until his death, their grandfather also shared their limited space. John Marsh lived in a one bedroomed cottage in Lower Mill Street. His sister slept in the sole bedroom with his parents whilst he and his brother slept on the landing until he left home in 1959 to get married. George Cox was born at 8 Raven Lane where he was brought up with his two brothers and two sisters. His sisters slept in one bedroom with his parents whilst the three boys slept in the only other bedroom. As for Winifred Howard, she lived in what had been Holdgate Fee but was then 120 Old Street. At the time of the Second World War Winifred lived there with her mother, stepfather and eight siblings. They had only two bedrooms so the eldest four boys slept in one whilst the girls and the young children slept with her parents. With so much of the housing stock virtually unchanged since the nineteenth century such conditions remained for many well into the second half of the twentieth century.

A further reason for cramped living conditions was because extended families often lived together. This could sometimes mean three or even four generations living in the same house. Before the advent of the welfare state, an elderly parent, who could no longer work or had been widowed, may no longer have been able to afford to remain in their own home or, because of low wages, a married couple, sometimes with a child, would have to stay with a parent or parents-in-law until they could afford to rent a house of their own. The prevalence of extended families living together can clearly be seen using the 1911 census. In Lower Broad Street four married daughters with their husbands and children lived with their parents; four different households also had grandchildren living with them, perhaps the offspring of unmarried daughters or, more likely, because their parents' home was too overcrowded; two homes had widowed mothers residing with the family whilst in four other households could be found a nephew or niece living, again perhaps because of overcrowding in their own home.

The same patterns of living can be seen in Lower Galdeford. Here seven households had married sons or daughters, together with their children, living with their parents. Four couples had elderly mothers or fathers living with them whilst another six couples or widows had grandchildren living with them. In two cases they were adult grandchildren. In addition, a further five households had nephews or nieces living with them.

Shared accommodation was also still prevalent after the Second World War. Eileen Jones and her brother, Bob (Rusty) Matthews, had, for a while, to share their house on St John's Road in the 1950s with their mother's brother, wife and young child until they could find a home of their own. This meant that Bob and his brother had to sleep on the landing on a mattress. In a cottage at the end of a small court, formerly known as Halford's Yard, entered by the side of 19 Raven Lane, Michael Newman shared two bedrooms with his parents and six brothers and sisters. Because of the overcrowding one and sometimes two of them had to sleep at their grandmother's, two doors away.

Yet another cause of crowded homes was a need to increase family income and to do this a number of households took in a lodger or lodgers. To find work many men had to go on 'the tramp'. That meant that at any one time there could be scores of workers looking for weekly or even overnight lodging in Ludlow. At the northern, lower end of Corve Street a number of households took in lodgers. At the time

LANE'S ASYLUM – OLD STREET

This 1895 scene of Lane's Asylum is interesting in a number of respects. For many years before the Victorian workhouse was built on Gravel Hill it housed the town's poor. Pavements were then cobbled rather than paved and the road laid with crushed dhustone from the Clee Hill quarries to give carts and horses a better grip when climbing up into town. Vagrants and itinerant workers produced much of this. In exchange for overnight board and lodgings in the casual ward at the workhouse, they had to break a certain weight of stone. The road going off to the right was Frog Lane (St John's Road) an area of poor housing where many hawkers had settled.

(Courtesy of Shropshire Museum Service)

of the 1881 census a widow and her family at No. 72 took in two boarders whilst next-door at 73 a widow and her father took in three boarders. Next door to them, at 74, a brother and sister took an entire family in as lodgers: a carpenter, his wife and two children. Just further up Corve Street at No. 89 a railway worker's family took in three boarders as did another widow and her family at No. 106. By 1911 nothing had changed.

Many families still needed the extra income lodgers could bring. The census then showed that in the cramped cottages of Lower Broad Street, lodgers could be found residing in six properties whilst in Lower Galdeford they could be found in twelve, usually just one man, though in one case a married couple were put up whilst in two homes three lodgers could be found in each. A typical example was at No. 35 where Robert Price, a nineteen-year-old auctioneer's clerk, was now the chief breadwinner after the death of his parents. He was responsible for his two younger brothers and four younger sisters aged between four and seventeen years. The eldest sister, aged fourteen, had to keep house. Even though they had only two bedrooms, in order to supplement the family income they took in a lodger who at the time of the census was a 75-year-old travelling jobbing tailor.

With so many men and even women travelling from place to place in search of work, and therefore of lodgings, regulation was deemed to be required. In 1851 Parliament passed the *Lodging Houses Act*. This Act designated two types of lodging houses: nightly lodging houses where the lodger paid by the night and those lodging houses where the lodger paid by the week. The nightly or common lodging house had, under the Act, to be registered with the local authority. This registration was then subject to annual review. A locally-appointed Inspector of Common Lodging Houses, as well as the police, had the right to enter such premises at any time. The weekly lodging houses could also fall under this legislation if the council passed the relevant byelaw, but Ludlow Council decided not to, which meant that they were free from inspection.

In the year 1865/66 Ludlow had seventeen common lodging houses registered and all were in the working class areas of the town: one in Old Street, six in Holdgate Fee, two in Lower Broad Street, one in Corve Street, four in Upper Galdeford and three in Lower Galdeford. These were licensed to lodge between four and twenty-two people at an average of ten per lodging house.[5] A glimpse of what lodging houses were like on the inside can be discerned from a report by the Inspector in January 1886. In four of the six properties inspected at the time three men were allocated to each bedroom. At 42 Holdgate Fee twelve men shared three bedrooms whilst at the largest common lodging house in the town at 1 Waterside, at the bottom of Holdgate Fee, twenty-four people shared just four bedrooms. Two premises required 'a thorough cleaning' being in 'a dirty condition' whilst two needed lime washing. This was to be carried out annually under the licence and was seen as a natural antiseptic and a deterrent to insects such as cockroaches. In two properties the bedrooms were deemed to lack fresh air as they had bricked-up windows while other windows just opened up onto another bedroom.[6]

Such lodging houses were seen as far from respectable and it was not just the lodgers who fell foul of the police. At 1 Waterside run by a couple named Pilson:

'During the last twelve months this house has been

QUARRYMEN

One expanding industry that brought local employment opportunities was that of quarrying in the Titterstone and Clee Hill areas. A number of Ludlow men were employed even though this meant at first a long daily walk from home to a quarry, many arduous hours wielding a hammer to break the stone, and then a long walk back. As the years passed cycles and buses were used to travel to work.

(Courtesy of Shropshire Museum Service)

very badly managed. Both Pilson and his wife are frequently drunk and quite incapable of looking after the house and the rough class of people they get there, and the police are frequently called there and have had a great deal of trouble.'

As a result the police recommended in 1900 that the licence should not be renewed. When the Town Council considered this request their deliberations shed some light on the numbers of itinerants passing through Ludlow looking for work. When deciding, against advice, to allow the renewal of the licence it was explained that, in their view, the closing of this lodging house would place an intolerable burden on the other lodging houses that could hardly cope as it was.[7] It remained open until the 1930s.

The mass of people passing through Ludlow looking for work is further emphasised by the numbers applying to stay in the casual ward at the workhouse. If those looking for lodgings either could not find or afford them then they could

THE TANNERY – LOWER GALDEFORD

This is the old Tannery in Lower Galdeford, finally demolished in the 1970s, along with residential properties either side, to make way for council homes. Both sides of Lower Galdeford saw backbuilding. Here, as well as the front doors to properties, could be found alleyways leading to cottages in yards behind. One can be seen on the far right of the photograph. (Courtesy of Shropshire Museum Service)

apply to the workhouse to stay in their casual ward. Here they would be bathed, fed and given a bed. These vagrants, as they were known, could be 'men of the road' or those searching for work. The numbers varied greatly depending on the state of the economy. 1861 saw 831 such men and women applying, whilst in 1880 2,547 requested overnight accommodation. During the interwar years of the twentieth century the casual wards at the workhouse on Gravel Hill were often full. In 1928 an average of forty vagrants a week were housed rising to seventy in winter. The beginning of 1938 saw 242 men and women admitted in the first five weeks. All were expected to work for their lodgings with men having to break dhustone, quarried on Clee Hill, to be used for road building, whilst women had to pick oakum though this had changed to general cleaning duties by the 1930s.[8]

The importance of this evidence of itinerant labour travelling through the town is that it highlights another factor about working class life: the absence of breadwinners in many local families. Numerous Ludlow men were forced to travel away from town in their search for work to support their families. Wives then had to fend for themselves whilst awaiting a husband's return or the receipt of a postal order. Sometimes the call would come to join their husbands in a far off town or city.

A number in Ludlow also became hawkers or pedlars again causing many to travel throughout the surrounding countryside in order to obtain a living. Under the *Pedlars Act 1871* such a person was defined as anyone who tramped from place to place carrying his goods or tools of his trade himself. From this date he, or she, had to apply to their local police force for a 5/- annual licence. In 1879 seventy-nine Ludlow residents were granted such a licence, twenty-one of them women. All lived in the poorer areas of the town. Visiting pedlars also had to show their licence to the police and have

PICKING OAKUM

As with these women pictured here, for many years female vagrants and itinerants, in exchange for one night's board and lodging at Ludlow's workhouse, had to pick oakum. This was the teasing out of fibres from old ropes and was very hard on the fingers. The loose fibres were then sold to shipbuilders for mixing with tar to seal the lining of wooden vessels.

it endorsed. Eighty-three did so in the year April 1879/80 and ninety-six the following year.[9] In 1881 the same system was extended to hawkers who were defined as persons who travelled from place to place with their goods or tools using a horse or other beast of burden. By the turn of the nineteenth century many of these hawkers lived in Holdgate Fee, Frog Lane (later St John's Road) and St John's Lane. A number of them were travellers who had decided to settle in Ludlow.

For those that found employment and made a living in Ludlow, wages were low and this in turn kept rents low and, as will be seen later, gave landlords a reason not to improve properties. Glove manufacturing declined from the end of the Napoleonic Wars and by 1850 Ludlow was a place of numerous small industries. A workshop of hatters could be found in Broad Street employing 8-10 men whilst in Lower Broad Street besom making (brooms made from coppiced birch and hazel) was carried on. In addition, 12-20 men found work in a woollen mill where the street met the river.

Rope spinning took place on land behind Friar's Terrace and parallel to Old Street, and about twenty men were employed making spade handles in the Linney. Five or six premises also employed coopers making cider casks and various dairy utensils for local farmers, whilst nail making also took place. This would be carried out in a workplace attached to a cottage or at the end of a garden or yard. It would contain an anvil, hearth and bellows and a workman could make one thousand nails a day whilst his wife or elder child worked the bellows and other children fetched and carried the coal for the hearth. However, maltings provided most work in Ludlow with up to 24 of them supplying local inns that brewed their own beer. Eight maltings could be found on the east side of Corve Street. By the end of the nineteenth century unskilled labouring was still the main employment for men in the town whilst virtually all the trades existing fifty years earlier had disappeared, with malting only just lingering on, having

LION MINERAL WATER WORKS

With the demise of the glove industry after the Napoleonic Wars no large new industry replaced it. As a result, Ludlow reverted to being the market town for the surrounding area. A myriad of small businesses now offered local employment and one of these was the Lion Mineral Water Works that was situated behind the Three Horseshoes public house at 5 Upper Galdeford. In addition to mineral waters various ales and stout were also bottled for local consumption. (Courtesy of Shropshire Museum Service) succumbed to the rise of national brewers. Taking their place was a gas works, an expansion of the building trade together with brickmaking, the opening of quarries on Clee Hill and employment on the railway. In addition, with the expansion of commercial trade as Ludlow continued to be a market town, there grew a need for more carters.[10] Very few of the jobs offered by these new or surviving industries offered high wages, whilst traditional work linked to agriculture, that after 1870, went into decline with the expansion of farming in the New Worlds of North and South America, Australia and New Zealand, still offered very low pay.

The beginning of the twentieth century saw little change especially as the economic doldrums of the interwar years brought no new industries to the town. The Rector of St Lawrence's outlined the extent of Ludlow's economic problems in 1937 in an address to the town council. He pointed out that two hundred men were registered to receive unemployment benefit, another one hundred were subject to the Means Test, which meant that unemployment pay was withheld until all possible assets or other means of support had been exhausted, and yet a further one hundred were receiving help in some form or other from the Board of Guardians or Public Assistance Committee. This meant that four hundred households in Ludlow out of 1,500 required some form of financial help: over a quarter of the population and a far higher percentage if just working class families are considered.[11]

The consequence of all these factors is that working class life in Ludlow remained hard throughout this entire period. As the following chapters will show, housing conditions remained spartan, incomes low and health poor.

CHAPTER TWO

Sewerage, Drains, Privies and Water Closets

In the mid-nineteenth century Ludlow still had its ancient sewerage system to which just a few of the larger buildings were connected. Under a Local Government Act of 1858, borough councils could form a Local Board of Health with the power to raise monies to carry out improvements. In Ludlow one such improvement was the building of a new sewerage system and between 1862-1866 contractors carried out this work. Houses could pay to be connected but the bulk of Ludlow's landlords did not do so, with the result that most of Ludlow's working class population throughout the nineteenth century, remained on what was known as the privy system.

Privies were usually small wooden or brick-built buildings with a wooden seat with up to four holes cut into it. The individual holes would be partitioned off from each other. Excreta would drop into a pail that, when full, could be buried as manure in the garden if the household had one or emptied into a nearby cesspit. At some properties excreta could fall directly into a cesspit or into a channel that connected with one. Most privies and cesspits were situated in the yards and courts that could be found throughout the town while some of the larger houses could have one in a cellar. The cesspits themselves could be up to 20ft deep. Their quality varied and they could be wood or brick-lined. Some would allow the urine to seep away and that would keep the pit relatively dry. Most cesspits in Ludlow had a wooden cover that could be removed to empty waste into them or to allow access when they were emptied. To keep the smell down and to speed up the drying process, ashes could be laid on top and then, after another layer of excreta was deposited, a further layer of ashes would follow. The pits could last for many weeks before they needed emptying.

However, some families did not even have the dubious pleasure of having a privy. Within the borough some landlords

FLOODING – LOWER CORVE STREET

Four yards or courts could be found on the western side of Lower Corve Street. As well as being narrow, dark and badly drained they were also prone to flooding from the River Corve. Here, in 1924, nearly all the ground floors of the properties find themselves waterlogged. At such times a trip to the lavatory, if possible at all, would need wellington boots. It was more likely that the sewers would overflow and human excrement would float in the floodwater. In the distance can be seen local residents surveying the scene from outside the Queen's Arms public house. (later renamed the Bridge Inn). A Mr and Mrs Houghton peer out of their door in resignation at the situation, an entrance to one of the number of yards along this stretch of street just behind them. (Courtesy of Brenda Oliver) would not go to the expense of providing one whilst, before the boundary was extended in 1901, a number of properties on the outskirts of the town had no sewerage system to connect to. This posed the problem as to what the residents should do with their human waste. Most of the new building in the suburbs had plenty of garden space attached that allowed for some of the occupants to dispose of the content of their pail closets by burying it. In the crowded and tightly packed properties in the old borough, this was often not an option. St Mary's Lane, off Corve Street, had a number of families in this position. Visiting Council officials in 1870 found it 'a deposit for filth of the worst description.' Five cottages, including one with twelve family members and another with nine, had no privies. James Pugh, who lived at number 3, said that he used the nearby orchard as his lavatory, whilst one of his neighbours, Mary Hicks, said that her family, along with others, 'go into the lane.'

Families living elsewhere in the borough were in the same position. Arthur Lowe, who lived at 80 Corve Street, said that his family went 'anywhere' whilst the tenant at number 87 used a tin bucket that he emptied at night in the street's open sewer. Jones' Yard in Upper Galdeford had no privy and residents poured their excreta down a grating in the street. Even a common lodging house at number 33 had no privy and again poured their excreta in the sewer via a grating. In a similar position was Davies' Yard in Holdgate Fee where 'filth' was 'thrown into the street nightly.'[1] It took until the end of the nineteenth century before the need for such actions were finally eradicated.

For those that did have privies, one of the resultant problems that they brought to plague the town was that the contents of the cesspits often seeped into the surrounding soil and from there into adjoining properties. This was not helped by the nature of the ground to be found in Ludlow.

The Medical Officer of Health (MOH) in his report of 1877 explained that the seepage from such pits into the surrounding soil was exacerbated by the fact that the local subsoil was very porous. One example was seen at Rogers' Yard in Frog Lane (later St John's Road) owned by Edwin Rogers the landlord of the adjacent Wheatsheaf Public House. Liquid from the cesspit, filled by the single privy that served four cottages, percolated through the soil and seeped through the walls of the nearest property. It did not help that seepage was increased by the fact that there was no covering to the cesspit and no guttering on any of the properties with the result that rainwater also drained into the pit. In addition, the residents also used it to empty all their slop water.[2]

Many cesspits constantly overflowed. This occurred if the privy was not emptied often enough or if the lid was not watertight or if there were faulty drains or even no drains at all. This would mean that waste water or rainwater could run into the pit. Such overflows kept the Inspector of Nuisances busy, for whenever one was reported he had to go out and inspect the relevant pit and press for remedial action to be taken. Such visits occurred virtually every week.

Again, cesspits with broken covers or none at all were partly to blame and the fact that many of the wooden covers were not repaired or replaced by landlords when they rotted did not help. The cover of the cesspit in the yard adjoining Lane's Asylum in Old Street was found to be in disrepair with the result that the tenants of the six surrounding cottages threw their slops in filling it even more quickly and stopping the excreta from drying out.

A similar sight of partly rotted covers that allowed both rainwater and household waste water to find its way into a cesspit could be found in the Nag's Head Yard and Drew's Yard (Nos. 2 and 3 Courts) off Corve Street. A number of pits had no cover at all such as in Watkin's Yard off Lower

LAVATORIES AND WASHHOUSES - RAVEN LANE

This rare view of lavatories, washhouses and back building behind houses on Raven Lane highlights the dark, ugly and cramped conditions that many working class people in Ludlow had to suffer. In addition, the roof of the nearest building is a reminder that many landlords failed to keep their properties in a good state of repair. As a result roofs often leaked and many cottages suffered from damp. A narrow alleyway, leading off the Lane to further properties, can be seen in the foreground with a door set in the nearest wall giving access to the back yard shared by the nearest property.

(Courtesy of Ludlow Historical Research Group)

Broad Street and in Dean's Yard off Old Street where the cesspit served eighteen houses.[3] Such an overflow of 'offensive matter' from a cesspool was also reported in Sheldon's Yard, Upper Galdeford. It was 'running on the adjoining premises so as to be of a great nuisance.' The owner of 95 Upper Galdeford also reported 'a drain of offensive matter' from the single privy that was shared by three neighbouring properties in the Greyhound Yard.[4]

Lack of drains often exacerbated the problem and caused further complaints. The lack of drainage in Frog Lane was always a constant cause of complaint. None of the cottages were drained with the result that the residents merely threw their 'refuse, offal and dirty water into the gutter opposite ... causing very offensive smells.' Such habits in turn caused further problems as regards sewage disposal. Refuse, thrown in the channels or 'kennels' that ran down the side of streets ended up being washed down the gratings or 'gulley holes.' Such channels and gratings were designed to allow rainwater

MIDDEN – COLLEGE STREET

Middens were accumulations that were often comprised of human and animal excrement, ashes and general rubbish. At a time when many houses did not have water closets, coal fires the norm for heating and cooking, and rubbish collection was in its infancy such piles were a common sight. They would be collected at intervals to be used by farmers as manure. This one was behind an old property in College Street in 1878. (Courtesy of Shropshire Museum Service)

to wash out the sewers but they now often became blocked. As the MOH explained to the council in 1898, this meant that the sewers could then back up and cause sewage to overspill into both streets and cellars. One councillor in 1900, who lived in Old Street, claimed that after a recent rainstorm his cellar was three feet deep in water and after it drained away he was left with three inches of raw sewage.[5]

The absence of drains also meant that many yards were in a constant filthy state. Those in Frog Lane had so much stagnant water lying in them that brick ends had to be laid to construct rudimentary stepping-stones that enabled the residents to walk from their back door to the privy. Taylor's Court, off Lower Broad Street, also lacked drainage and was in a similar state. Dirty, stagnant water continually gave off an offensive smell and the area was described by the Inspector of Nuisances as 'one of the worst drained, filthy places in the borough.' In Tower Street, the King's Arms Yard was also not drained and 'offensive water allowed to run on to the street' whilst Number 1 Court in Old Street was often flooded with raw sewage. The problem was widespread throughout all the working class districts of the town.[6]

Where drains had been installed they often blocked and many landlords failed to maintain them. This was a cause of discomfort and annoyance not only to the tenants but to others. As was explained, when a drain became blocked in Lower Broad Street, this caused 'a soak of offensive matter to flow in a cellar adjoining' and meant that the contents of a privy had to be 'carried in buckets to the sewer to the great annoyance of the neighbours.' The yards of public houses

OLD STREET BEFORE CONSTRUCTION OF THE CLIFTON CINEMA

This Georgian property on Old Street, owned by William Price, the head of a family plumbing firm, was demolished to make way for the Clifton Cinema that opened its doors in 1937. Though some felt this damaged the street scene it should be known that behind this building had been one of the worst slums in Ludlow: Dean's Yard. Here eighteen homes once shared just two privies and both these once lacked doors. All the cottages had been emptied and declared as unfit for human habitation as early as 1901 but they still remained as a rotting eyesore. Next to it was Noakes Yard with fourteen cottages, another notorious slum that had slowly been emptied in the first quarter of the twentieth century. The coming of the cinema finally removed these two blights from the town.

(Courtesy of Shropshire Museum Service)

could also be a problem because of the use of a single privy by their customers. At the Star and Garter in Corve Street, when the drain was blocked the yard was 'covered with filth of the worst description through not using the privy which is scarcely fit to enter.'[7]

The shared use of privies was not just confined to public houses. Because of the cramped conditions in the yards and courts of Ludlow, very few working-class homes had a privy to themselves. At Deans Court off Old Street, the

LOWER BROAD STREET, LOOKING UP. c1880

A lack of proper drainage was a problem for many residents. This was Lower Broad Street c1880. Note the open drain running down the side of the street with occasional covering flagstones to help pedestrians to safely cross. The theory was that rainwater would flow along the drain and on entering the sewerage system would help flush it and keep it clear of obstructions. What happened is that residents, lacking drains in their houses, would pour their slops and deposit waste in the public drain. This, at times, brought about blockages. After a severe rainstorm, this could then cause the sewers to back up and overflow into the street or flood cellars leaving behind inches of human excrement. (Courtesy of Shropshire Museum Service)

NEW ROAD SUBURB

This photograph of the top of New Road shows some of the new working class terraced homes built in the 1870s and early 1880s by the building firm of Weales in the East Hamlet area of the town. Though of far superior quality to many of the homes in the centre of Ludlow the lavatory facilities, though one per property, were in other ways inferior. Being outside the borough boundary this area was not on the sewerage network. This meant that the houses were on the simple pail system that had to be emptied each week. It was not until after the borough boundaries were extended in 1901 that this area could have water closets. At the top of the street can be seen East Hamlet School opened in 1877.

(Courtesy of Shropshire Museum Service)

tenants of eighteen homes had to share just two privies and in 1865 even these two were in a terrible condition, one lacking both a door and a seat whilst the other only had part of a door remaining. No doubt the wood had been scavenged for fuel. In Lower Mill Street four of the cottages had to share a single privy and that too was in a bad state of repair. It was the same in Sheldon's Yard in Upper Galdeford where 'there are no doors to the privies.' Privacy when relieving yourself was far from easy to come by and the numbers attempting to use the same privies perhaps explains some of the filth in yards, passages and even streets as both men and women could not or would not wait for a privy to become vacant. By the start of the twentieth century the situation had not changed for many. In Lower Mill Street ten adults and thirteen children still shared a single privy whilst in Page's Yard, Upper Galdeford the families of eight cottages shared just three privies.[8]

A further discomfort that had to be faced was the emptying of the cesspits. This was a job for the night-soil men who tended to work in groups of four. As their name indicates their work was carried out whilst the residents were in bed

BULLS HEAD TOILETS

It was not only houses that had outside privies or water closets for the same was true of public houses and shops. The courtyard of the Bull Hotel (c1900) held their lavatories seen here on the left. At least patrons only had a short distance in which to brave the elements and a well-maintained path to cross unlike many public houses in working class areas. Many would only have one to be used by both men and women. Poor drainage often caused these to become blocked whilst patrons often would not wait for the sole lavatory to become vacant and relieved themselves in the yard.

(Courtesy of Shropshire Museum Service)

and less likely to have to endure the stink caused. The men obviously preferred a dry cesspit where rain or waste water had not found its way in and where the urine had drained away as wet cesspits just made the job more difficult as well as more odorous. One man, the hole-man, climbed into the pit and filled a tub, then a rope-man pulled it up whilst the two remaining men placed the tub on a pole and carried it to the waiting cart. Ludlow had two of these 'sludge-carts' but with the demand on their services the night-soil men were constantly falling behind in their work.

After complaints as to the smell from the cesspit in a yard at Lane's Asylum in Old Street that served six cottages, the owner defended himself by claiming that he had asked for it to be emptied but that it took two months for the night-soil men to arrive. They then admitted to him that 'we have more orders on hand than can be attended to.' As a result, a third 'sludge cart' was purchased in 1905 so that prompter removal could be guaranteed and the work finished by breakfast.[9]

Removal of excrement when the population was beginning its day had been a cause of complaint. A letter to the Town Clerk in 1903 described the consequences of the late removal from a cesspit situated in No. 2 Court, Upper Galdeford. It was claimed that it was:

'Frequently emptied between the hours of 7 to 8 in the morning and the state of the contents (semi liquid) is of such a nuisance as to poison the air for a considerable distance from the seat of the complaint. The remark of the people living in the neighbourhood is 'we can smell it in our beds.' Those whose misfortune it is to have to pass by at the time are in a position to use stronger language.'[10]

The carts took the night-soil away and emptied it on a number of sites. Up until 1908, among other places, this waste was dumped at Burway, Felton, the Sheet Road near Dark Lane, and Ludford Park. Between 1895-1903 some was also taken to the Smithfield adjoining Lower Galdeford and

RAIN BUTTS – NEW STREET

When these new working class houses in New Street were built c1880 they were just outside the borough boundary and, therefore, not connected to the borough's drainage system. As a result, as can be seen, the drainpipes emptied directly into rain butts to save the rear of the houses being flooded. By 1923 when the Jackson family lived here, the landlord had still not carried out any improvements. The rainwater collected in the butts would still be used each morning or evening for a cold strip wash. (Courtesy of Geraldine Sadler)

Weeping Cross Lane that was, at that time, being used as a rubbish dump and after this to a new rubbish tip at Portman Meadow, Fishmore.[11] At all these sites it was mixed with other rubbish including ashes, road sweepings, animal dung and rotting vegetables to be sold as manure to local farmers.

The lack of an efficient sewerage system that all houses in the town could connect to and which could cope efficiently with its effluent disposal, held back the widespread introduction of water closets in the town since their installation would cause a large increase in the amount of effluent. As it was, the MOH criticised the state of the two sewerage outlets at the Linney and on Temeside in his 1897 report and warned the council that inaction could have legal consequences.

'The present system is very bad and thoroughly inefficient. The tanks themselves (80 years old) are objection-able and the effluent passes into the river chemically untroubled in any way... The present system constitutes a grave violation of the River Pollution Act.'

ROAD – LUDFORD

With tarmacked roads and maintained pavements it is difficult to imagine the filth that our forbears once had to walk through. This c1880 view of the road into Ludlow, just before it passes over Ludford Bridge, gives an indication: a glutinous mixture of mud and animal dung. In parts of Ludlow itself slop water and even human excrement could be added to the mix.

(Courtesy of Shropshire Museum Service)

He recommended that all the sewage should be taken to just one outlet, Temeside, downriver of the borough, and treated properly by precipitation and filtration. The MOH also gave examples as to how the present system was not adequate for many properties within the borough.

'*The open sewer running from the top of Lower Galdeford towards the Friars should be done away with and a proper sewer laid. There should also be a sewer laid at the bottom end of Corve Street for the houses adjoining the river to drain into.*'

Recent building on the eastern boundary of the borough was also causing problems. Raw sewage had contaminated the watercourse from St Julian's Well, and the stream from Sheet Road to the Weeping Cross was also now polluted with sewage from the Gravel Hill district. He saw both as a health hazard to the town.[12] As a result the council at last acted and a sewerage improvement scheme was begun in 1900 and virtually completed in 1902 when it was also decided to extend the new system to the East Hamlet area that had just been incorporated into the borough.

Landlords were now asked to do away with privies and install water closets and connect them to the new pipes but, since this was not compulsory, at first the take-up was slow. In 1907 there were still 497 privies in use in Ludlow. Since it is estimated that there were 1,000 working-class properties in the borough, added to the fact that many families shared privies, then it is clear that, notwithstanding the recent new sewerage system, the overwhelming bulk of homes remained on the privy system.[13] The council was initially spurred on to encourage, persuade and even contemplate forcing landlords to install water closets by an embarrassing disclosure following a letter to the Town Clerk from a concerned citizen about the state of privies at Upper Galdeford.

'*The conditions under which the tenants have to live seems to make it imperative that water carriage should be resorted to as a means of ending the nuisance. Your Sanitary Committee appear to make spasmodic attempts to deal with similar cases, but on complaining to the Inspector in this instance, he informs me that the cottages in question are the property of a member of the Sanitary Committee.'*

The landlord was, in fact, William Chubb, who lived with his wife and two servants at 3 Brand Lane, and he was not just a member of the Sanitary Committee but its chairman. Newspaper editorials now began asking probing questions about the inner workings of the council.

'Is it true, for instance, that the property was condemned a few years ago? If so, what improvements were carried out to justify a revocation of the closing order? Was the condemnation withdrawn by the Sanitary Committee ... and by whom?[14]

Such pressure appeared to work. Shortly afterwards the council asked the MOH and the Inspector of Nuisances to make a list of all properties in the town not on the water carriage system. They also put pressure on landlords to convert to water closets by threatening to levy a charge for emptying cesspits. Once the first lists were received, the council began sending out notices to landlords insisting that they install water closets. 63 notices were despatched between February and April 1908 with this figure reaching 328 by the end of the year. As a result, by December 1912 only 106 privies remained in the borough reducing to just 12 by 1920 when legal action was finally threatened.[15]

As Ludlow moved from privies to water closets this did not mean that the sharing of such conveniences ended. Admittedly, a few landlords took the opportunity to increase the number but many families found themselves, half a century later, still sharing a lavatory and, with them being outside, they still had to walk or run to use them in all weathers. After the Second World War, at the Brickyard, each terrace, one consisting of five houses and one of six, still had a single lavatory whilst most cottages in St John's Road shared one

ST JOHN'S ROAD

This is St John's Road in the early 1960s. This had always been a poor area, being, at times, the home of nailers, laundresses and hawkers. Municipal improvements were often slow to reach such streets. In 1865 it was said that 'they have no water except at the river, neither is there any drain laid for them to the main sewer ... (it is) consequently a deposit for every sort of offensive matter.' When the properties were finally demolished in the mid 1970s many of the residents were still sharing lavatories and outside water taps. After demolition the road was widened, the wall on the left lowered to just two foot in height and the land behind it turned into a municipal garden. (Courtesy of Shropshire Museum Service)

'down the yard.' Living in Raven Lane, Michael Newman recalls that the four cottages in his yard shared two lavatories whilst the family of Angie Clare and Alice Pound shared a lavatory with their neighbours in the Central Hall Yard, Upper Galdeford. Quiller Robertson's maternal grandmother, who lived on the Linney, shared one with her neighbour whilst Winifred Howard, who spent her childhood in one of a block of four cottages at the bottom of Old Street, again shared two back-to-back lavatories. Situated by the side of a path that ran behind the cottages, even though they had been converted to water closets, they still retained the original wooden seats, being a bench with holes cut into it.

Wherever you lived certain etiquette was always observed when using these shared lavatories. As Les Fury explained, even though there may be a row of four lavatories for the use of eight cottages, as in the Greyhound Yard, you only used the one allocated to your family. If it was already occupied by a member of the family that you shared it with, even though others may have been vacant, you did not use any of them.

THE VINEYARD

The Vineyard is a row of cottages off the west side of Lower Broad Street. Originally one-up, one-down properties as shown in this c1900 photograph, they had been condemned as unfit for human habitation prior to the First World War. Their shared lavatory and washhouse were at the far end of the terrace. The original cottages remained inhabited for many years and survived until they were purchased and renovated as late as the 1980s.

(Courtesy of Lottie James)

As he pointed out: 'You used one: you kept to one.' This was an unwritten law as David Weaver, who lived in Portcullis Lane, confirmed:

'Even when you went up to the loo and someone slammed the door, you thought Christ! You'd go back down and use the bucket behind the door in the back kitchen.'

Since many lavatories only had a thin partition between them, some family members were loath to use theirs if a neighbour was using the one next to it. In such cases Elfreda Sampson explained what used to happen. *'We used to watch. "Mr So and So is coming out of the toilet now. You can go in."'*

Since the lavatories were all outside and none were lit, at night families tended to use a chamber pot kept under the bed. At Steventon Road, where Jean Parker lived, the chamber pots were emptied into a slop bucket each morning and then carried out to the lavatory that was to be found halfway up the back garden. At the home of Winifred Howard in Holdgate Fee, a similar morning ritual was followed. Here it was the job of the eldest boys to empty the pots or pail. Quiller Robertson's grandmother on the Linney had a commode in her bedroom but when Quiller stayed with her, instead of going upstairs with an oil lamp after dark, she was told to squat over the slop bucket in the scullery. Freda Stewart recalls that the lidded slop or chamber bucket, when not in use, often contained soiled towel nappies being soaked before boiling.

As for lavatory paper, old habits died hard. All those interviewed remembered using old newspapers cut into squares, threaded on to a piece of string and hung by the side of the seat. Brenda Oliver joined her mother to carry out this weekly chore. *'That was our Sunday afternoon job. Putting it on a string.'* Winifred Howard's mother sometimes treated her family by going up to town and collecting paper that had been wrapped around apples and oranges. *'She'd bring a bagful home and string them up. That was our soft paper.'*

Since 1850 little had changed as regards answering the calls of nature for most working class people. Admittedly, water closets had at least replaced privies but lavatories were still outside and that often meant an uncomfortable windswept and sometimes rain-sodden trip into the yard or down the garden path. They were also still often shared which meant an uncomfortable wait at times, whilst squares of newspaper inside still sufficed for cleansing. At night nothing had altered, with chamber pots and pails still in constant use. Even by the advent of the Beatles many working class families in Ludlow still could only dream of having their own indoor lavatory.

CHAPTER THREE

Water and its Domestic Uses

By 1851 Ludlow's drinking water supply had altered little since the 12th century. Then it was piped to the castle from a spring in Whitcliffe Woods and brought to the town by gravity. By the mid-nineteenth century this system also served a conduit behind the Buttercross. In addition, another conduit, situated in Corve Street, just below what is now Station Road, was probably supplied by a spring on Gravel Hill whilst the White Conduit, to be found at the Tolsey in the Bull Ring, was fed by a pipe from St Julian's Well. Yet another conduit was situated in Galdeford.

These conduits supplied the drinking water for the bulk of the population of the borough. Each day a family member would have to walk to the nearest one in order to fetch and carry back home whatever amount was required. The better-off sections of local society would, no doubt, send a servant to do this work whilst a few of the larger properties may even have had their own private well. Ludlow's growing population, however, meant that this water supply was becoming under increasing pressure. For example, the cistern at the conduit at Galdeford was no longer large enough to satisfy demand by 1863, so a new 2' pipe was run to Lower Galdeford ending in a communal brass tap.[1]

The result of this growing shortage of drinking water was that by the mid-nineteenth century, Ludlow had developed a dual system. Water for everyday domestic chores such as personal washing, the washing of clothes and cooking was supplied by a separate system supplied directly from the River Teme. At the beginning of the 19th century a pumping station was built at the bottom of Mill Street, complete with turbines, and it supplied the town with 7,000 gallons a day. River water was pumped to two large reservoir tanks on the north side of the Market Hall in Castle Square as well as being piped underground into a number of Ludlow streets to serve pumps from where the local populace could more conveniently fetch it. For an annual charge to the council, this water could also be piped directly into a property and several of the wealthier citizens took advantage of this.

Nearly all of the street pumps and taps, however, were within the old walled town, but it was outside these walls that the majority of the poorer sections of the community lived. As a result, it was not until the 1860s and early 1870s that these

DOLLY TUB

Each of the terraced houses in New Street, built c1880, had a lavatory at the end of their 40-50ft garden. In addition, they had a brick built wash-house in the yard outside the back door. Here, in the 1920s, can be seen a long line of them: one for each house. Water from the coal-fired boiler would be ladled into a dolly tub containing the washing and this was then agitated using a three-legged wooden dolly, here being used by a young Phyllis Jackson. In the yard, alongside a rain butt, could also be found the cold-water tap. (Courtesy of Phillip Sadler)

ELAN WATER PIPELINE

This scene (c1900) shows the construction of an aqueduct two miles west of Ludlow to carry a water pipeline from the newly constructed Elan Valley reservoir in Wales to Birmingham. At this time Ludlow often experienced water shortages when rainfall was low with the town's water supply often having to be reduced to just a few hours per day. Once this pipeline was opened in 1907 an arrangement was made with the water company to purchase supplies for the town in times of drought.

(Courtesy of Shropshire Museum Service)

families had easier access to water. In Frog Lane (now St John's Road) complaints were being made about 'filth of a disgusting nature' that was accumulating in the street that 'principally arose from the want of supply of water.' The residents had to walk to the river to fetch their water and, after such an effort, they would be loath to use it to wash away waste.

Finally, in 1865, the council ordered that water taps be placed at each end of the lane though householders would still have to walk uphill to the centre of town to collect drinking water. A similar situation existed in nearby Lower Broad Street and it was 1868 before street pumps were installed to supply the residents with river water. Then in 1870, for the first time, they also got a communal tap from which drinking

GREYHOUND YARD

Up until 1937 the house on the right was the Greyhound public house situated where Upper Galdeford met Gravel Hill. Until the area's demolition in the 1970s, the entrance that led to the Greyhound Yard could be found next to it. Here eight terraced cottages with a row of four outside lavatories still stood. Built in the mid nineteenth century their water was still supplied by an outside water tap. However, when Les Fury moved into one of cottages in 1957 the landlord of his property had just supplied the luxury of a cold-water tap in the corner of the living room over a simple open drain in the floor. (Courtesy of Shropshire Museum Service)

water could be obtained to save them walking to the top of Broad Street or to the Bull Ring. Holdgate Fee (the lower end of Old Street below Lane's Asylum) received its first water pump in 1871.[2]

Such a system could not survive and disease unlocked the door to improvement. As has been seen, a new sewerage system was installed in the borough between 1862-66, but it was based on having two outflows discharging raw sewage into the River Teme: one at the Linney and another at Temeside. Since the former was upstream of the pumping

Water & its Domestic Uses

station at Lower Mill Street, the effect on public health was soon a major concern. Between September 1875 and June 1876 over thirty cases of typhoid were reported in Corve Street and by the end of the year this figure had risen to 85. The wealthier local inhabitants demanded that the council should act. No agreement as to the cause of the outbreak could be agreed upon but a firm of London Water Consultants, Gotto and Beesley, were asked to write a report on Ludlow's water supply. Their findings were damning.

'The supplies piped into the houses are supposed to be used only for cleaning and domestic purposes but as all potable (drinking) water has to be brought from street taps, it is not unreasonable to

HOT BATHS FOR 2d

In the interwar years, the Ludlow Gas Company, with their main shop then situated in Broad Street, were advertising baths for the price of 2d when a gas heater supplied the hot water. Since many families could not afford the installation costs and most landlords were happy to leave facilities in their properties as they were, then the weekly bath in a tin tub in front of the fire still remained the norm for many in Ludlow. (Courtesy of Ludlow Historical Research Group) *suppose that this river water is in many cases used for drinking; and when it is shown that the point of the river from which the water is taken is a short distance below the point of discharge from the sewage tank ... It is obvious that the source is objectionable and prejudicial to the public health.'*

They stated that the river as a source should be abandoned at once, as should the use of the ancient wells and local springs since they too were now becoming polluted by excreta, partly due to houses being built higher up the slopes than their outflow. At the same time, after reports of the typhoid outbreak reached the Local Government Board of Health in London, an inspector, a Dr Airey, was despatched to investigate the state of sanitation in the borough. He too reported that the dual water system should be ended and that a new single water supply that was drinkable be constructed.[3]

After a great deal of debate, mainly concerning the scale of increased costs to the ratepayer, a scheme devised by a Timothy Curley was chosen. He proposed to use the water from the Boiling Well Spring on the Burway and have it pumped up to a reservoir on Whitcliffe which, it was claimed, would be high enough for sufficient pressure to enable fresh water to be delivered to the whole of the borough and, in addition, to the workhouse on Gravel Hill which was just outside the borough boundary. Until this point the inmates were dependent on water drawn from their private well that often dried up after a period of little rain, with the result that boys and men had to be sent down to the river to carry supplies back up the hill.[4]

In addition, new turbines and pumps were installed at the bottom of Mill Street so that river water could be extracted and pumped to the Whitcliffe reservoir at times of drought with the hope of ensuring a constant uninterrupted supply. By June 1880 all householders in Ludlow were asked to connect to the new water mains if they wanted water in their home and on 1 September the river supply was disconnected. At the same time the conduits that had supplied fresh water to the populace for many years were discontinued.

Because the scheme covered just Ludlow borough this meant that the new houses that were being built in the Parish of East Hamlet in the 1870s and 1880s were not being supplied and had to rely for water on newly-dug wells. As regards the working classes, this meant those living in the new terraced property on New Street, Chapel Row (later renamed Belle Vue Terrace), Dodmore Lane and along the New Road. Once again the impetus for change was the fear of disease.

In the autumn of 1884 an outbreak of typhoid on the outskirts of the town had 'attained the dimensions of an epidemic.' Thirteen houses were infected and eleven of these were in what is now Belle Vue Terrace, a row of sixteen

ALLEYWAY - 43 OLD STREET

Buildings behind those fronting the street were common throughout the town. Here, in 1951, is an alleyway by the side of 43, Old Street (now the Wonder House Takeaway) that gave egress to No. 41 on the left. The property on the right has since been demolished. In 1914, further back behind these properties could be found the Plymouth Brethren Chapel (later known as the Gospel Hall) and a handful of cottages in what was named the Chapel Yard. These all now lie under the Clifton Court car park. As can be seen, washing lines had to be erected wherever a householder could find the space. This could be difficult in shared yards and often laundry had to be dried in a downstairs room in front of the fire.

(Courtesy of Shropshire Museum Service)

CONDUIT AT THE TOLSEY

This engraving shows drinking water being collected in buckets from a conduit situated at the Tolsey in the Bull Ring. Known as the White Conduit the water was piped from St Julian's Well. It was not until the 1860s and early 1870s that working class districts outside the town walls were given access to fresh water through occasional street pumps and taps. Until then they had to walk to the nearest conduit in the centre of the town or use polluted river water. (Courtesy of Shropshire Museum Service)

houses. The other two infected homes were close by. The Medical Officer of Health (MOH) of the Rural District Council (RDC) blamed a contaminated well that served all the houses. The drain from the house first infected ran within a few feet of the well and he believed that water from the wringing out of linen that had been contaminated by excreta was the cause.[5] For some time the RDC had been asking Ludlow Council to supply water to this outlying part of the town and now, at last, they agreed. By 1890, this had been carried out.

A similar situation arose in Ludford Parish with the building of new working class homes such as at Steventon New

Road. In 1898 a fresh outbreak of typhoid, which this time encroached into Ludlow itself, was traced to contaminated milk from Foldgate Farm, Ludford. The cause was identified as a leaking privy next to a water pump. Once again, health fears moved Ludlow Council to listen to requests to supply this bordering district with mains water.[6]

But although a water supply was being connected to all parts of the town this did not mean that all houses had a water supply. The overwhelming bulk of the working class population in Ludlow were tenants and many landlords would not, or claimed they could not on financial grounds, pay to have their properties connected to the mains. What they did, either acting on their own or with other landlords, was to put taps into the many enclosed yards and courts that littered the town or behind terraces. These were then shared by a number of households. The council played its part by ensuring that all streets had a water main with Portcullis Lane finally getting one in 1909. As a result, by 1914, virtually all the pumps and taps that previously had been placed in the town's streets or in the larger courts for communal use, had been removed though the occasional cast iron pump could still be seen in 1960.

The sharing of a water tap was widespread throughout the working class areas of Ludlow and how common it was can be seen in its survival into the second half of the 20th century. The MOH for the borough, in his report for 1947, stated that in Lower Galdeford 70% of the properties had no inside water source of any kind.[7] Oral evidence shows that this was not just limited to Lower Galdeford. When Elfreda Sampson moved into 33 New Road, the end house of a terrace of six, the only water came from an outside tap in the centre of a yard that ran behind the houses. An open gulley ran the length of the yard to drain away waste water and as her house was the last one on the downward slope she had to keep it clean. A close friend of Elfreda's lived at the Brickyard at the lower end of New Road.

Here could be found two rows of terraced cottages, one of six and one of five, and each terrace had just one outside tap. At 85 Lower Corve Street Brenda Oliver's family had to share a tap with numbers 86, 87 and 88 as well as with a property on St Mary's Lane behind. Bob Jones, brought up in St Stephen's Yard, Upper Galdeford, remembers his family sharing an outside tap with six other cottages. The experience of the sisters Alice Pound and Angie Clare, who spent their childhood in Central Hall Yard off Upper Galdeford, concurs. They lived in a terrace of four cottages that shared one outside tap. This they were still doing when they left in 1959. When, in 1951, Joe Griffiths moved to his first marital home at 10 Rock Lane, one of a block of eight back-to-back houses, he and his wife also found themselves sharing a communal tap.

Back in the centre of town, Les Fury, whose father had a boot and shoe repair shop at 119 Tower Street, recalled the six cottages in Weaver's Yard behind them also having to share a single tap. It was the same at the lower end of Old Street. Winifred Howard lived in the end cottage of a row of four. None had running water inside but shared a single outside tap behind the row, whilst Freda Stewart's family shared the one tap in Grieves' Yard off Holdgate Fee (entered by an alleyway to the side of No. 3, later 95, Old Street) with three other families. Lower Broad Street held yet further examples including the nine cottages in Taylor's Court (reached by an alleyway between numbers 22 and 23). Margaret McGarrity, who lived at No. 7 remembers that all the families shared the one tap.

Sometimes, even reaching a communal tap was not easy. In 1955, those living at 34 and 35 Lower Raven Lane, whose landlord was the Governing body of the Ludlow Grammar School, had to cross the school playground to collect their water from behind other school-owned cottages on Silk Mill Lane.[8] When a landlord wanted repossession of 10

ALLEYWAY, c.1960 (THE SNICKETS)

In 1850 Ludlow had a dual water supply system. In addition to drinking water that could be obtained from the public conduits, river water, to be used for everyday purposes, was available from water pumps situated in most streets. Once a single water system was introduced in 1880 these pumps were slowly replaced over the years by simple, shared, outside taps. However, a few of the original cast iron water pumps still survived in 1960 and one can be seen here in an alleyway off Corve Street that has since been renovated and is now known as 'The Snickets.' (Courtesy of Shropshire Archives)

Upper Galdeford he offered the tenant a cottage on the other side of the road that had another cottage attached to its rear. The move was refused partly on the grounds that, in order to access water, the family would have to exit the front door that faced the main road and then go down an alley at the side to the shared yard behind and then retrace their journey.[9]

As we saw with Angie Clare and Alice Pound, even as late as 1960 working class families with no water inside the home and sharing an outside supply was still a common occurrence throughout the town. Being outside, the tap was also liable to freeze in the winter. In Portcullis Lane, Denis Weaver's parents would often have to light a fire under the communal tap in order to defrost it, as did Susan Jones' mother at Rock Lane. Freda Stewart, during her childhood in the 1930s, recalls the council having to bring a communal water tank to Holdgate Fee when the outside taps froze during particularly harsh winters.

A few landlords improved their property by installing a cold water tap inside but when they did, it was often very simply done. When Les Fury moved into his first marital home in the Greyhound Yard off Upper Galdeford he found that the landlord had attempted to modernise the house by partitioning off a corner of the living room and putting in a cold water tap over a simple drain in the floor. One of his first jobs was to install a sink.

Far more often it was the tenants who installed water at their own expense. David Weaver's parents had cold water piped into their house in Portcullis Lane in 1950 and soon afterwards their neighbours did the same. However, the tenants of the other three houses in the terrace could not afford this and so carried on sharing the outside tap. Joe Griffiths,

SHOP – WASHDAY

A number of the wares on display in the interwar years outside Roberts the ironmongers, at 55 Broad Street, give clues as to how housewives carried out their weekly washing. On the left are piled galvanised dolly tubs with a lip on them to rest the soap. To the right of the shop-front are tin washtubs of varying sizes that would soon adorn the back walls of cottages waiting to be used for rinsing the boiled laundry or for the weekly bath in front of the fire. (Courtesy of Ludlow History Research Group)

ST JOHN'S ROAD – BACKYARD

This is the rear of 13 St John's Road c1955. Hanging on the wall either side of the back door can be seen the tin baths that were used on washday for the laundry and on bath nights, in front of the fire, for the family. Such a sight could be seen at the rear of most working class cottages. Note also the state of the brickwork and also the lack of paint on both the window and doorframes. Many landlords failed to keep their properties in a good state of repair, often claiming that it was not financially feasible to do so considering the low rents received.

(Courtesy of Eileen Jones)

on moving into his first home in Rock Lane with his new wife in 1951, using his own labour, installed a sink with a cold water tap, his property being the only one in a block of six to have such a luxury. When Elfreda Sampson moved into 33 New Road with her husband in 1942 they, along with three of her neighbours in the terrace of six, clubbed together to have inside taps installed. The remaining two families still carried on using the one in the yard.

Water was, of course, needed for the washing of clothes and household linen. This was usually heated in a 'copper' boiler that was actually made of cast iron and encased in brick with a small fireplace at the bottom which could be lit using wood or coal to heat the water. The boiler would take about six buckets filled from the nearest tap. These 'copper' boilers were often situated in a purpose-built washhouse. The newly-built terraced houses being erected on virgin development

THE MANGLE

Scenes such as this would be a common sight on washdays in many parts of Ludlow. Mangles were used to squeeze water out of newly washed and rinsed clothes and this was a task that required a lot of manual effort. Since this labour was normally carried out in the backyard, a home made lean-to was often constructed to protect the housewife for when it rained. Not all families had such a modern convenience as a mangle and would have to borrow the use of one from a next door neighbour or just wring out the washing by hand which would have been even more strenuous.

land on what was then the outskirts of Ludlow, such as New Street, Belle Vue Terrace etc., were each given their own washhouse. In the crowded yards and courts of the borough, such outbuildings, when a landlord provided them, often had to be shared. Margaret McGarrity and Daphne French recall that the houses in Taylor's Court and Whitcliffe Terrace, both off Lower Broad Street, shared a washhouse. Nos. 4, 5 and 6 Lower Mill Street, a small terrace situated behind the properties that faced the road, also had to share. It was the same at 80, Lower Galdeford where the mother of Joan Thomas shared one with two neighbours.

Sharing a washhouse brought its own problems. The occupants of the two terraces of five and six houses in the Brickyard off New Street which each shared a single washhouse had to come to an agreement as to their use. As Elfreda Sampson explained, *'They had to work it you see for one to use it and then clean it out for another to use.'* It was the same with some of the houses in Page's Yard off Upper Galdeford as Joe Griffiths recalls. Again neighbours had to agree as to which day was their washday.

Arguments could break out if it was felt that agreements had been broken. One was so serious that two women found themselves in court. They were Mary Jones, who lived with her husband above their tailor's shop at 27 and 28, Bullring, and Susan Goodwin who lived in one of the four cottages in the yard behind (now rather grandly named Attorney's Walk). All five families shared a communal washhouse. Mary's day for washing was Tuesday but this time she claimed that she found the washing tubs, shared by her neighbours, inside the washhouse and in her way so she moved them outside. Susan Goodwin claimed that Mary Jones did not use the washhouse every Tuesday but when she did she always asked one of her neighbours to move the tubs, which they always did. This time she did not ask and Susan took exception to this and a fight ensued. That such arguments were commonplace can be seen when Mary Jones' solicitor informed the court that:

'This storm over the washtubs was one of those squabbles which so frequently occurs when there was only one washhouse used in common by several tenants.'[10]

The washing of laundry could take a whole day. The fire under the 'copper' had to be lit first thing in the morning after filling it with buckets of water from the tap. Once the water was heated, some of it was ladled out into a wooden or galvanised iron or zinc tub and into this were placed the coloureds to soak. Whites were left in the 'copper' and boiled. After soaking, the coloureds were often agitated from side to side using a three-pronged dolly stick and then scrubbed, using carbolic soap, on a wooden washboard with a corrugated zinc surface in order to get the dirt out. All washing, both coloureds and whites, had to be rinsed several times. The clothes and linen were lifted out of the tub or copper with the dolly or wooden tongs and then put through a mangle. This was a crank-operated gadget that squeezed excess water from clothes by pressing them between rollers. This was to get rid of as much dirty, soapy water as possible before the laundry was put in an oval galvanised 'tin bath' for rinsing. This bath had handles for carrying and for hanging on the yard wall when not in use. Clothes were put through the mangle again after every rinse. Finally the laundry was hung out to dry outside on a clothes line if the weather was fine or placed on a clothes rack in front of the fire if wet.

Many homes, however, did not even have a purpose-built washhouse. Their 'copper' would be in their back scullery or, more likely, set against the rear of the property covered by a homemade lean-to. This was the case at 8 Lower Mill Street, the home of John Marsh; at 35 Lower Broad Street, the home of Sheila Stephens; and at 120 Old Street, the home of Winifred Howard.

Water & its Domestic Uses

EAST HAMLET SCHOOL – WASHDAY

This is Edna Parsons nee Barber and Maureen Edwards nee Caulfield at East Hamlet School c1952. It highlights the fact that it would be expected at that time that girls such as these would one day be expected to carry out the physically tiring, washday duties for their family in exactly the same way as their mothers and grandmothers before them. As well as the tin bath and pail, note the scrubbing board for getting any stubborn dirt out and the wooden clothes horse on which washing would be dried in front of the fire on wet days. (Courtesy of Steven Edwards)

Yet many homes in Ludlow did not even have a 'copper' boiler to heat water on washday. As a result, for these housewives, washday was even harder. Marilyn Weaver's mother, who lived in Market Street, had to heat her water on washdays on top of a gas cooker before pouring it into a galvanised bath tub that sat on an upturned wooden box. Having no mangle, she also had to wring out her clothes by hand. When finished, Mrs Weaver 'chucked the water all over the yard and with a hard broom she scrubbed it until you could eat your food off it.' When Marilyn married in 1957 and moved into a flat above 1 Market Street, she too had to heat her water on a gas cooker and do the washing in the sink. As for drying, this had to be done in one of the bedrooms.

Doreen Lewis and her husband moved to Lower Broad Street in the mid-1950s. On washday, having no 'copper,' the water had to be heated in a two-handled galvanised tub on top of the gas cooker. When the water was hot enough, the tub was placed on the kitchen table and the laundry washed by hand. It all also had to be wrung by hand as she had no mangle and if it was wet, the clothes were dried in an upstairs room. Winifred Howard's mother in Old Street also had no mangle but 'next-door had and if her husband was out,

WATER PUMP AT THE BOTTOM OF MILL STREET

For most of the nineteenth century Ludlow had a dual water supply system. Drinking water was collected from the handful of conduits or from pumps and taps that were gradually placed at irregular intervals in surrounding streets from 1860. Water for all other uses was supplied from the river by a pumping station built at the bottom of Mill Street at the beginning of the nineteenth century. This supplied 7,000 gallons daily to numerous street pumps or, for an annual charge, directly into a home, though only the wealthier inhabitants could afford this. Since sewage was emptied into the river upstream of Mill Street, a new single water supply system was introduced on 1 September 1880 after a number of health scares caused by polluted water. The pumps were then used to top up the reservoir on Whitcliffe in times of drought.

(Courtesy of Shropshire Museum Service)

the neighbour would let Mum use it.' Sharing a mangle was quite common. At Joan Thomas' house not only were her immediate neighbours allowed to use her mother's mangle but also her extended family that lived in nearby houses in Lower Galdeford. They would bring their rinsed washing over to Joan's backyard in a metal tub.

Washday meant hot, steamy, physical work over many hours. Sheila Stephens, whose childhood was spent in Lower Broad Street, summed up those days when other household chores such as cooking had to be put on hold.

'I used to hate washdays – three lines down the garden and stew for dinner and I hated stew... It was horrible. The home smelt of washing.'

Washdays also had a number of unwritten rules. If washing had to be done on a Sunday the clothes were never put out to dry on that day. As Susan Jones explained: 'It wasn't the thing ... They had to have some pride.'

After clothes were dry, ironing was the next job for the housewife. In the majority of households this too had changed little by the mid-twentieth century, with metal flat irons still being used. At least two irons were needed: one in use and one re-heating on a trestle fixed to the cooking range. It was another hot, arduous task and the irons had to be kept meticulously clean and lightly oiled so as to avoid rusting. Constant care was needed to ensure the irons never got so hot that they scorched cloth. Many housewives could tell the correct temperature simply by spitting on the hot metal or by holding it close to their cheek.

A number of those interviewed describe ironing carried out on a table in the kitchen or living room with a blanket over it for protection. It was not until well into the second half of the twentieth century that most working class homes in Ludlow received electricity, and only then could electric irons be used.

For some women, carrying out their own washing and ironing was not the end of such labours. Before a laundry opened in Corve Street in the interwar years, most middle class families would put out their washing to a laundress. These were often widows or single women who had to support themselves and their children. The 1861 census for the Old Street Ward, which encompassed the working class areas of Lower and Upper Galdeford, Tower Street, Old Street, Holdgate Fee, Frog Lane, St John's Lane and Friar's Lane, shows the numbers involved. Twenty-two heads of household were listed as washerwomen whilst a further 32 were noted as charwomen, some of whom, no doubt, would bring home laundry as part of their duties.[11] This had hardly altered by the 1911 census. In Frog Lane alone (now St John's Road) three heads of household, two widows, one with a daughter, and one a single parent with two children, were listed as laundresses. In addition, two others were given as charwomen and two as housekeepers who, almost certainly, would have laundry to do for their employers.

Even in the mid-twentieth century some middle-class households used such women to launder their linen rather than send it to a laundry. Winifred Howard's mother, who had eight children, had to work as a charwoman to bring in extra income. She would go to work at 5.30 each morning to clean out the fire grates and re-lay them and do whatever washing up was needed from the night before. Once this had been completed she would bring the heavy washing, such as bed linen, back to her cottage in Old Street to launder. Michael Newman's mother in Raven Lane also took in washing and ironing from middle-class households in order to supplement the family income.

Personal washing had its own difficulties, as many Ludlow working class families did not have the use of a bathroom until well after the Second World War.

Consequently, ways of keeping the body clean was another aspect of working class everyday life that had hardly changed from the mid-nineteenth century. Since cold water, more often than not from an outside tap, was the only water available, this meant that washing most days was only cursory. Most of those interviewed described having a 'bowl wash' in the scullery with water heated on the range or the cooker if they had one. All eleven in Freda Stewart's family had such a wash each morning. The home in Lower Galdeford where Joan Thomas lived did not even have a scullery. Their daily bowl wash was carried out on the scrubbed wooden table. Some interviewees even remembered just having a cold wash that sometimes took place at the outside tap. In the evening it was the same except that most then had a 'strip wash.'

A bath was enjoyed just once a week at a stipulated time on a Friday, Saturday or Sunday evening. With no bathroom, this was usually taken in the tin bath used for the laundry that between times was to be found hanging outside the back door. Winifred Howard, who had eight siblings, described her family's Saturday bath night that, for warmth, was carried out in front of the fire. The youngest ones bathed first, the others in order of age. The same water was used. It was just topped up now and again with a fresh pan of hot water. Meanwhile, there was the fear in such large families that someone might urinate in the water before you got in especially since, as Susan Jones pointed out, that hair was washed in the same water you bathed in.

Privacy was also difficult but had to be coped with. In the Howard household, the eldest boys bathed in private when all the other children were in bed whilst in the Swindell's household Angie Clare and Alice Pound recall their father departing to the nearest public house every Friday evening whilst they and their two sisters had their bath before the fire. Parents would usually bathe when all children were in bed.

Even though Joan Thomas lived in a small one-up one-down house she recalls that during 'all my years at home as a girl, I never saw my father undressed.' To preserve some modicum of modesty, baths were sometimes taken in a bedroom even though this necessitated a number of trips upstairs carrying buckets of hot water. Freda Stewart and her three sisters would bathe in the tin bath first, followed by her five brothers. Such scenes would be repeated in many working class households throughout Ludlow.

For some in the 1950s there was an alternative. After John Marsh and Don Burmingham began to earn a wage they, on a weekend would go to a house down an alley at the top of Old Street in which a mother and daughter lived. On the first floor were four baths in separate cubicles that could be hired. Sixpence paid for the hot water though you had to bring your own soap and towel. John recalls that he usually had to clean the bath first since the previous user often left a dirty ring. The alternative for Jean Taylor in the early 1960s, since her home in Upper Galdeford had no bathroom, was to go to her grandparents' council house on Steventon Crescent for a bath, instead of using the tin one in her cold kitchen. When Jean married in 1973 and left home, her mother, still in Upper Galdeford, then came to their house for a bath.

An Act of Parliament of 1846 had allowed local authorities to obtain loans to build public baths and communal wash-houses to provide facilities for people to have a hot bath and launder their clothes. Many towns and cities took advantage of this but Ludlow never did. There was just a belated attempt to have one built in 1949. In this year the council passed a resolution to try to have a swimming pool constructed, but one councillor asked for a wash-house and bath-house to be included in the project pointing out that: 'Many women would think us angels if we could get public wash places for them.' His call fell on deaf ears.

Once the old dual water supply was ended in Ludlow, very little changed as regards access to water for most working-class families. A shared water tap in the backyard was for most the norm whilst a few had a cold tap inside in the scullery. Just a very few by 1960 had a small gas geyser installed to heat water, whilst a hot water system was still a dream for the overwhelming majority of families living in the older cottages that made up the bulk of the housing stock in the borough. As regards the washing of clothes, ironing and personal washing, very little had changed for the bulk of Ludlow's population in one hundred years.

CHAPTER FOUR

Housing Conditions

As was seen in Chapter One, the late 18th and early 19th century saw an expansion in the building of poor quality working-class housing that culminated in the many Yards and Courts that littered Ludlow. This was a result of infilling behind the properties that fronted the existing narrow medieval street system. When the long term decline in agriculture set in from the late 1870s, much of Ludlow's working-class housing stock was already nearly one hundred years old and some up to two hundred years. With much of it quickly and cheaply constructed in the first place, the time for its improvement or even demolition had been reached.

However, a number of factors militated against this happening causing their further deterioration through the first half of the twentieth century and beyond. The result was that many families lived in slums that became the breeding ground of disease and a cause of poor health.

In the last decade of the nineteenth century, the Medical Officer of Health (MOH) highlighted the decline of the quality of the housing stock, and its effect on the families who resided there. His report for 1897 starkly stated:

'I am sorry to say there is a large proportion of cottage property in the borough which is a disgrace for any town, and it is generally admitted that these unhealthy and dilapidated dwellings have a damaging effect on the moral status of the inmates.'[1]

Housing Conditions

This thinly-disguised attack on the council's inertia regarding this problem was remarked upon again in his report the following year. He complained that many councillors saw the attention that he drew to the matter as 'authoritively fanciful and needlessly alarmist.' To his voice was then added that of the editor of the *Ludlow Advertiser*. An editorial noted that:

'There is property in the borough, which has been considered as unfit for human habitation, still being utilised as dwelling places. .... Sadder still, there is not a member of the Town Council who dares lift his voice against such a palpable injustice.'[2]

CENTRAL HALL YARD

Off Upper Galdeford in 1975, this group of cottages and the Labour Club on the left, together with lavatories, old washhouses and the backs of properties facing what was known then as the Tin Yard on the right, was originally called Page's Yard. When plans for its demolition were being discussed in the 1970s it was known as the Central Hall Yard. Further down the alleyway could be found another terrace of four one-up, one-down cottages and their outbuildings. (Courtesy of Ludlow Historical Research Group)

HOLDGATE FEE

This is Holdgate Fee (now part of Old Street) in the 1960s. Being outside the old town walls this had always been a working class district. The properties fronting the road suffered some back-building behind them. The picture is taken from where the Old Gate stood and the road to the right is St John's Road (originally Frog Lane being built along the side of the town moat). All the properties on the right, a number of which had been deemed unfit for human habitation as far back as the first quarter of the twentieth century, were finally demolished in the 1970s to make way for council homes and sheltered accommodation. (Courtesy of Shropshire Museum Service)

Excuses now start to be voiced by the Sanitary Committee as to why so little was being done to try to improve the situation. They said that they tried to act regarding each individual case that came before them but many landlords, often widows for whom such property had been purchased to insure them against poverty in old age, could not afford what was asked of them. Also, to embark on a slum clearance scheme would be wrong. It would mean that the council would have to rehouse all those made homeless. In turn this would mean borrowing more money than they could afford whilst at the same time trying to pay for a new sewerage system.³ At times, councillors hid behind the byelaws claiming that as none had been broken, their hands were tied. This they did when Councillor Bishop complained about the state of a property on the Linney owned by Lord Windsor.

*'I don't know whether you allow people to live in barns; it is not even that, for a barn has a dry floor and here you have, sleeping on the floor, a man and woman and several children.'*⁴

There were even a number of councillors who would not admit that Ludlow had slums. Though Councillor Marsden claimed that *'some of the slums in Ludlow would compare very unfavourably with the slums in their large towns'* and that *'there was a good deal of property ... that was in a very bad state,'* others

LOWER BROAD STREET c.1890 LOOKING DOWN

Up until the last quarter of the twentieth century, Lower Broad Street had always been a working class area of the town. In the mid-nineteenth century the street was the centre of besom making: brooms made from coppiced birch and hazel. It also had a woollen mill down by the river that employed up to twenty people. In this view taken in c.1890 note the number of cottage windows that are open. This is because most cottages had another built to their rear so that the only fresh air or light they received was from the street. (Courtesy of Shropshire Museum Service) disagreed. Alderman Thomas Atherden, a retired banker, who lived in some comfort with his family at 27 Broad Street, looked after by a cook, two housemaids and a kitchen maid, would not admit that Ludlow had slums.

'Though there was some old property in the borough, he did not think it could be compared with slums in some towns … He did not know of any particular slums in the borough that they could sweep away with prudence if they were so inclined.'

In fact, he went on to assert, in regard to the families living in such properties *'it was, in his opinion, a bit of a blessing as well as a curse, because if they had modern dwellings people would have to pay extra rent and there were plenty of people who could not or would not do this.'*[5] It will be seen that many of these arguments would be reiterated by councillors over the next half century as housing conditions for many families got progressively worse.

However, the council were finally forced to take some action by the Local Government Board (LGB) in London who had read the annual MOH reports. As a result, in 1912 the MOH was asked to carry out an inspection of all properties on a district-by-district basis, with the first being Galdeford. The Sanitary Committee was soon given his damning report on 35 of the first houses visited. He pointed out that:

'The chief defects found were in regard to cleanliness, lighting, ventilation, paving and draining of yards, want of a proper food store and general dilapidation of floors, walls, ceilings and stairs. The majority required extensive repairs and alterations to make them sanitary and several of them in courts off the main streets can never be made satisfactory in regards to ventilation and lighting.'

He discovered that many properties were damp and some admitted rain through holes in their roofs. It was recommended that a number of them, that had passed the point of being improved, be demolished.[6] Sadly, the First World War

Housing Conditions

intervened and gave the council a reason to postpone action, though the MOH carried on making his inspections. By 1921 55 houses in Lower Galdeford alone had been condemned as unfit for human habitation but all were still occupied due to a lack of alternative housing. It appears that because many of the houses were built on a downward slope, there were examples *'in which people were living a yard underground. They were more like rat holes than houses.'* And such ruinous property was not just in Lower Galdeford. In a one-up, one-down cottage in Taylor's Court off Lower Broad Street, a newly-widowed woman with three young children had to suffer the rain coming through her roof and dripping on the body of her husband as he lay in his coffin awaiting burial.[7] A solution was at hand but was

MILL STREET

Behind the respectable façade of many of the streets of Ludlow was hidden another world: one of slums and poverty. Mill Street was no exception. In 1931, by the side of the house on the far right, an investigative reporter from the Ludlow Advertiser found a narrow, covered passageway that led to Maund's Yard. Here, families survived in a number of small, cramped, dark, dilapidated cottages that suffered from sagging ceilings and damp walls. Cottages on which, it was claimed, the sun never shone.

(Courtesy of Shropshire Museum Service)

COTTAGES IN ST MARY'S LANE

The poor quality brickwork and the rotting window frames of these cottages in St Mary's Lane gives an indication of the poor living conditions still being suffered by many in 1960. Though condemned up to fifty years before, the delay in building council homes to rehouse the residents meant that such cottages were saved from demolition since there were no other properties to move those displaced to. In the meantime, there was no incentive for landlords to improve such properties since either they claimed that they could not afford to do so or it was felt that the cost could not be recovered through increased rents. (Courtesy of Shropshire Museum Service)

not grasped. As we will see later, although the council were instructed to build the first council estates under the *Addison Housing Act 1919*, they again approached this solution very tentatively indeed. It took until after the Second World War before the provision of council houses to help solve the town's housing problem was seriously attempted.

The result was that, in the first half of the twentieth century, much of the working-class housing throughout the borough became more dilapidated as the years passed.

In 1930 a visitor from Tenby to the town expressed his shock at what he saw.

'On my first visit to your beautiful old-world town I was delighted with the old type of black and white houses and the castle and the beautiful church, all of which stood in the centre of the town. But, seeking the by-ways, I came upon some of the worst type of slum dwellings which nauseated me.'

He then went on to ask why the local council was doing nothing to rectify this disgraceful state of affairs.[8] Things came to a head again after the government passed the *1930 Housing Act*. This specifically encouraged local authorities to build council houses to rehouse slum dwellers but Ludlow council voted not to take advantage of it on cost grounds for at least three years. The Rector at St Lawrence's was incensed and delivered a sermon on the subject. He told the congregation, no doubt to the discomfort of many seated there, that:

'Home should be the happiest place in the world but this could never be while men were not provided with these homes. There were many houses in Ludlow which it was a misnomer to describe as a home – they were hovels ... How could they sit down in peace and listen to the church bells play 'Home Sweet Home, there is no place like home' while they knew that a hundred yards away people lived in these hovels where pools of water poured through the roofs. ... I have got a pair of eyes to see these things and they are not right'.[9]

In addition, letters began to arrive at the local newspaper office. A resident of Shrewsbury wrote that *'I spend a large part of my time in Ludlow and one has been filled with horror at the distressing (a mild word) conditions under which so many people are compelled to live.'* Councillor Channin, who had been on the losing side of the vote not to build any more council houses in the near future, penned:

'While canvassing in Lower Galdeford one wet night in October, I was invited into one of the houses. The mother and her

UNICORN INN AND COTTAGES

This section of Lower Corve Street surrounding the Unicorn Inn had four small courts leading off it. This photograph from 1962 shows the continuing poor state of many of the buildings in what was then a working class area of the town.

(Courtesy of Shropshire Museum Service)

GREEN DRAGON YARD
OFF LOWER CORVE STREET

This is the entrance to the Green Dragon Yard (No. 4 Court) off Lower Corve Street in 1962. It can still be found between Nos. 91 and 98. The inn's landlord, Samuel Heath, built the first three cottages in 1772 and by 1900 this had increased to seven. The floor holds clues as to the lack of drainage these properties originally had. Though when photographed it was laid with a mixture of cobbles and bricks, the original pattern can be seen of a footpath with an open drainage channel to take slop water and waste into the main street where it would join yet another, larger open drain before finally entering the sewerage system through a grating. (Courtesy of Shropshire Museum Service)

son were sitting either side of the fire, and between them was a bath catching water which was coming through the roof and the bedroom above.'[10]

As a result the *Ludlow Advertiser* decided to send a special investigator to search out slum housing in Ludlow and report back on what was found. The reporter found that very many houses, often *'hid away from the sight of the average passer by'* were unfit to live in, and concluded that *'I have seen this week hovels that no man has a right to condemn his fellow man to live in, and conditions that the average, decent, living citizen would not tolerate for a day.'* The first cottage visited was one of eight properties that formed Maund's Yard in Mill Street[11] which shared three outside lavatories between them.

'Here, near the lower end of the street, we can find a long dark passage that seems to lead to nowhere in particular except it be the backs of the houses in the street. But, passing through, we come into what can only be described as an alley and there are eight houses huddled together. If the sun ever shines on Whitcliffe then I am positive it never penetrates this alley.'

One property entered had just one room downstairs and one upstairs and the roof leaked so badly that every time that it rained the residents had to get out of bed to find tins and pails to collect the water that dripped in.

'*A father, mother and three children live (there) and all five sleep in the only bedroom. Neither of the rooms are large enough to 'swing a cat around.' One has to bend to go in at the only entrance to the place. Standing in the middle of the room, in which every domestic task has to be performed, one need not extend an arm to its full length to touch the ceiling. Upstairs the bedroom ceiling is V-shaped and can be touched at the sides by extending an arm whilst lying in bed. And, shortly, in these surroundings, another young life is to enter the world.'*

In most of the cottages the lack of light meant that 'one has to peer closely at objects to distinguish what they are, and so dark and dreary are they that in some cases it is difficult to see what the pictures on the wall represent until one becomes accustomed to the darkness.'

Then Lower Galdeford was visited and here was found a property where there were six children with their parents.

'For over two years the roof has leaked every time it rains necessitating the people getting out of bed to move it to a dry spot at another end of the room.

The living room, owing to the damp on the walls, was devoid of wallpaper and I asked where the stairs were by which one went to the bedrooms. I was led to what was called the back kitchen and the floor had no concrete or tiles, simply the earth visible. The stairs were nothing but steps that a farmer would use to go from a stable to the hay loft.'

However, what was described as the worst spectacle of housing was in the Linney.

'*The scullery, where all the domestic labours of the house were performed, was worse than a stable; in fact any farmer with a true sense of his animals would not house his horses or cattle in such a place if it were given him rent-free. ... The roof showed in nine different places holes as large as a dinner plate and the sky could be seen. In fact the only light penetrating the place was the light streaming in from the holes in the roof.*'[12]

Faced with all this publicity the council, as they had already done before the First World War, were forced once again to ask the MOH to prepare a list of insanitary properties within the borough. Even so, some councillors like Alderman John Langley, a local coal merchant, still believed that the housing problem was being exaggerated. As a result he was invited by the investigator to visit some of the houses. The invitation was not taken up.

'*We leave the public to judge why he refused to see what he alleges do not exist. Very soon he will get a list sent to him officially, and then he will get the surprise of his life.*'[13]

A surprise it may have been, but little action followed. A sense of déjà vu permeated the council chamber in 1937 as yet more visits to Ludlow homes to assess the extent of the housing problem were embarked upon and history once again was repeated. Members of a sub-committee inspected just over fifty homes, and 90% of the tenants reported '*that they could not remember any money ever being spent on their houses since they had been there, and some of them had been tenants for fifteen to twenty years.*'

There was an attempt to argue for a minimum standard for all houses and if a landlord could not match this then the council should condemn the property. To achieve this the Health Committee recommended adopting model byelaws set out in the *Housing Act 1936* but was vetoed by the full council. Councillor Richard Poyner argued that the model byelaws were too severe and that if they adopted them then '*half the houses in Ludlow would have to come down.*' The same arguments were trotted out to avert further action. A great many people,

Housing Conditions

MILL STREET, c.1950s

Over the years as stables, carriage storage space and accommodation for grooms became redundant many were converted into workmen's cottages for renting out. As a result slum housing could be found alongside grand properties of yesteryear and even important public buildings. The Guildhall on Mill Street, pictured here in the 1950s, contrasts starkly to the more dilapidated buildings below.

(Courtesy of Shropshire Museum Service)

especially the old, would be unable to pay any higher rents and it could also cause great hardship to some landlords. It would mean *'ruination to poor people who had a bit of property and were living on the rents.'* Though Councillor Maxwell claimed that such arguments were *'no reason why these people should continue to live in the shocking, filthy and disgusting conditions they are living in'* he found himself outvoted. [14]

Once again war intervened and gave councillors yet another excuse to do nothing, though those who had the responsibility of housing evacuees now saw working-class living conditions first-hand. Yet again, a few concerned councillors described to their fellows in the council chamber examples of the suffering of individual families. Councillor Keyse:

'Knew of one case of a married couple with three children living in two rooms measuring roughly 11ft by 8ft. No window would open and there were rats there. Immediately off the living room was a place where the wife did the washing. To enter the house the occupants had to ascend a wooden ladder that was almost vertical and up and

down which all the water used in the house had to be carried. The washing had to be dried in the living room. There was one lavatory for five houses. The place was a rabbit hutch and a deplorable place for children to be born in.'[15]

When Jean Taylor's mother moved into a house on Holdgate Fee during the Second World War whilst her husband was in the forces, she found that she could see from one room into another though cracks in the wall. Rather than the landlord, it was her brother, a general builder, who had to carry out the repairs and replaster the property. Jean also recalled a childhood friend in Holdgate Fee whose scullery still had an earth floor in 1960.

As before, the stimulus to action came from without.

HOLDGATE FEE (NOW OLD STREET) – UPHILL VIEW

This early 1960s view northward, up what was once called Holdgate Fee, is interesting in that it appears to show that some houses had more than one front door. In reality one of them would most likely give access to another one or two cottages built to the rear together with outdoor lavatories and a washhouse that they would share with the properties facing the road.

(Courtesy of Shropshire Museum Service)

As the war drew to a close each council was instructed by the government to prepare a house-building programme for when peace came. Prodded into action, Ludlow now put forward plans that included council estates to be built on three fields adjoining Dodmore Lane, and nine acres at the rear of Sandpits Playing Fields.[16] Homes were built but their numbers were still not enough to solve a problem that had been allowed to fester and gain so much ground over so many years. And old habits died hard.

In 1953, after the Borough Surveyor had visited over 250 homes in order to compile a report on unfit housing as part of a possible slum-clearance programme, the council once again voted to take no action and shelve the scheme. However, it had to be resurrected when, under the *Housing Repairs and Rents Act 1954*, the council were ordered to set out how they would solve their slum problem. Advised by the Borough Surveyor and the MOH, the council, in 1955, was forced to list 206 properties that required demolishing, a figure that starkly highlighted the housing problem that still remained in Ludlow. This included 15 houses in Rock Lane, 7 houses in the Old Brickyard, 17 houses in Corve Street and St Mary's Lane, 21 houses in Mill Street and Lower Mill Street, 18 houses in Lower Broad Street, 28 houses in St John's Road and Lane, 38 houses in Old Street, 35 houses at Upper Galdeford and 44 properties in Lower Galdeford.[17]

Many of those listed were the same ones that had been found unfit for human habitation prior to the First World War, a fact that emphasises the very poor conditions that many families in Ludlow still had to endure. Furthermore, the scale of the problem was compounded by the fact that, in addition to these properties, there were many others still in need of major repair.

Vermin

And it was not just structural defects and lack of basic amenities that tenants had to suffer. It was also vermin and infestations. In 1922 a tenant went to court to fight an eviction order on the grounds that the alternative property that the landlord offered was a 'filthy place. It had no back kitchen (and) was overrun with rats and black beetles.' That this was seen as nothing out of the ordinary was shown when the magistrate granted the eviction order on the grounds that the property offered in Upper Galdeford was 'reasonable.' It was during the interwar years that one of the local unofficial sports was to hunt rats on the council rubbish tip. One Sunday, the mayor counted seventy people taking part with fifty dogs. The rat problem in Ludlow was so bad that the local newspaper complained that:

'There are many areas in the town infested with these destructive pests ... Hundreds were disturbed recently in connection with the destruction of some old buildings, only to find a new home.'[18]

In 1933 the Rector was moved to write to the council regarding a 'pest of rats on Corve Street' demanding that something was done about it.[19] After the Second World War rats were still a problem. In Holdgate Fee, Jean Taylor recalls that it was quite usual to see rats in the shared yard. In the late 1950s, Angie Clare and Alice Pound recall rats in their coal cupboard under the stairs in their Central Hall Yard cottage. Once trapped, clubbing with a poker by their father killed them. 'You should have heard them squeal.' Don Burmingham, on moving into 18, Rock Lane with his newly-wed wife in 1956, described it as *'one-up, one-down and as many mice as you could get... As soon as you heard the trap click you threw the mouse on the fire and set it again.'* One way of attempting to discourage rodents in homes was discovered by Ann Donnelly when carrying out improvements in St John's Cottage on

St John's Lane. The space between window height wooden panelling and the wall was found packed with broken glass. When this was mentioned to the estate agent on selling the property in 1968, Ann was told that this had been quite a common deterrent in Ludlow, especially for rats.

Rats were not the only infestation that residents had to suffer. In the 1930s, Councillor Violet Packer also noted that many of the fifty properties she visited with colleagues from the Sanitary Committee were infested with 'fleas, bugs and beetles.'[20] Even after the Second World Wars things were not much better. Margaret McGarrity, who lived in Taylor's Court off Lower Broad Street, recalled that all food had to be kept covered:

'...because the house was running alive with cockroaches. It was terrible. You had cupboards on the wall which you put your shoes and things in when you came home from school and then you moved something and they came crawling.'

JACK'S FIELD

Jack's Field, situated between St John's Lane and Old Street, was the last working farm within the borough boundary and milk from the cows here was still being ladled out from churns to local households in the third quarter of the twentieth century. What is interesting to note are the rear of the buildings facing on to Old Street (formerly Holdgate Fee). On the left can be seen two cottages built onto the back of those facing the street. In addition, can be seen two single floor scullery additions. Some of the ground floor rooms of these houses still had earth floors when they were demolished in the 1970s. (Courtesy of Shropshire Museum Service)

In Holdgate Fee, Freda Stewart vividly remembers cockroaches in her scullery.

'*Our Dad used to put stuff all over the floor: a powder. We used to sweep them into the coal house and then put them on the fire.*'

Lighting

Most working class cottages also still did not have electricity in the 1950s. They relied on gas lighting aided by oil lamps and candles even though Ludlow had got an electricity generating-station as far back as 1906. It was built on Portcullis Lane and initially fed mains throughout the centre of the town. Though middle and upper middle class homes were soon taking advantage of this, since the owners could afford the connection costs, most landlords of working class properties either could not or would not afford such an expense. This meant that fifty years later, many working class properties in the centre of Ludlow were still lit by gas, oil lamps and even candles.

Sheila Stephens, who spent her childhood in Lower Broad Street, recalled that her home had just one gaslight set on the wall at the side of the sink. For the rest of the downstairs, and for upstairs, oil lamps or candles were needed until the landlord finally installed electricity in the 1950s. Michael Newman's home in Raven Lane also had a sole gas mantle on the ground floor. This often needed an oil lamp to be lit to supplement the meagre amount of light given off. Candles were used upstairs. The same situation existed for Joe Griffith's home in Central Hall Yard, Upper Galdeford, as it did for David Weaver in Portcullis Lane, John Marsh in Lower Mill Street, Susan Jones in Rock Lane and Freda Stewart in Holdgate Fee. All just had a single gaslight whether they had one or two rooms downstairs. For some families, paying for

Housing Conditions

even this small amount of gas was difficult. Winifred Howard, who lived towards the bottom of Old Street, spoke of her mother having sometimes to just rely on oil lamps downstairs to save spending on the single gas mantle in the front kitchen. For light upstairs they used very small oil lamps that were 'just enough to see where you were going.' If they wished to read in bed then candles were lit. Brenda Oliver, whose home was in Lower Corve Street before moving to a new council house in 1949, did not even have gas lighting let alone electricity. Oil lamps and candles were all they had. It was the same for her neighbours as it was for Joan Thomas who lived in Lower Galdeford. Her family lived in a cottage that had neither gas nor electricity. The only light they had was from oil lamps or candles. Even when Joan moved into her first marital home at Rock Lane in the late 1950s, she found the same. It was only when she and her husband joined with her two neighbours to pay for gas to be installed that oil lamps could be discarded.

COTTAGES – LOWER GALDEFORD

Lower Galdeford had some of the poorest housing in Ludlow and was causing concern before the First World War. Still standing and inhabited after the Second World War, these cottages were typical of the dire standard of accommodation in this area. They were also the first to be demolished when an access road was required to Walters Trouser Factory that was situated between Lower Galdeford and Old Street. The alleyway in the centre led to one of the eight yards built at the rear of the properties facing that side of the street. It would also lead to a shared outside tap, lavatories and washhouse.

(Courtesy of Shropshire Museum Service)

CORNER OF UPPER AND LOWER GALDEFORD

Just outside the old town walls can be found the confluence of Upper and Lower Galdeford. In these two areas, where backbuilding was common, could be found many yards and courts and, especially on Lower Galdeford, some of the poorest housing in the borough. On both roads, for the entertainment of inhabitants, could also be found many public houses and, in the nineteenth century, brothels.

(Courtesy of Shropshire Museum Service)

For her, electricity was still in the future.

The use of oil lamps and candles could be a fire hazard, and accidents, sometimes fatal, occurred. Examples from the early weeks of 1876 show how common such accidents were. In a property backing onto Pepper Lane, a mother and daughter died from smoke inhalation from smouldering bedclothes caused by a candle. Shortly afterwards a two-year-old child in Lower Galdeford was seriously burned after his clothes caught fire, and a girl in Upper Galdeford set fire to a window blind whilst carrying a candle up to bed. Three more examples

Housing Conditions

from the twentieth century suffice to show the continuing danger. In 1922, in Lower Mill Street, a woman died after setting fire to her clothes when using a candle to light her way to the coal shed. 1930 saw a fire in Lower Galdeford when the occupant fell asleep leaving a candle burning by the side of the bed. In 1948 an elderly woman was found outside her home in Lower Broad Street with her clothes on fire after she fell whilst carrying a paraffin lamp to bed. She died from shock caused by her burns.[21]

As can be seen, by 1960 the condition of working class homes in central Ludlow had altered little since the nineteenth century and it could even be claimed that in some ways conditions had grown worse. Admittedly, access to water had improved somewhat and the privy system had been replaced

76, LOWER BROAD STREET DOORWAY – 1955

Marge Fallows, holding her baby son Lesley, stands at the backdoor of 76, Lower Broad Street in 1955. The condition of her rented property can be discerned though it was far superior to that of numbers 73, 74 and 75 that shared their small rear yard. The Medical Officer for Health and the Borough Surveyor had, for some years, deemed them unfit for human habitation. In 1954, under pressure from the Ministry of Housing, the council finally listed them for demolition in a future slum clearance scheme along with a further 233 homes in the town. They still stand today.

(Courtesy of Gail Fallows)

by water closets though these were still outside the home, but, as the years passed and landlords invested little in any other improvements, the stock of traditional working class houses had deteriorated. Council inertia, especially during the interwar years, had far from helped and, as a result, for many in Ludlow, poor housing was still the norm.

CHAPTER FIVE

Health and Health Care

One of the overriding, abiding concerns that can be discerned in most of the annual reports of the local Medical Officer of Health (MOH) is that of the poor health of Ludlow's working classes. This showed itself in the many diseases that were prevalent. Some of these were occasional visitors to the town such as cholera, typhoid and smallpox, whilst others, such as tuberculosis, scarlet fever and diphtheria, were constant, frightening companions. In addition, the general squalor that permeated the courts and yards in so many parts of Ludlow, added to the very limited health provision available to the bulk of the population, was another permanent concern being voiced, all of which was constantly reflected in the high death and infant mortality rates.

Typhoid

Typhoid is a disease that is linked to those living in poverty as a result of poor sanitation and poor hygiene, and is spread by eating or drinking food or water contaminated with the faeces of an infected person. Families in Corve Street fell prey to it in September 1875 with a total of 85 people succumbing to the disease within twelve months. Typhoid again visited the town in 1884 when thirteen households, eleven of them in Chapel Row, were struck down. As was seen in Chapter 3, both outbreaks led to improvements in water supply. The disease, however, was not eradicated and smaller outbreaks still occurred with, for example, three cases in 1899.[1]

Smallpox

Smallpox was the most feared disease. Between 20-60% of those infected died, whilst with children the death rate was

AUCTION YARD

In 1885 a private animal market was set up on land between Corve Street and the railway station. By c.1916, when this photograph was taken, it had put the municipal market, situated on the Smithfield from 1861, out of business. What it did mean, however was that livestock, mainly cattle and sheep, would be walked along Ludlow's streets each week until well into the second half of the twentieth century. Local children would take advantage of the cows left overnight by going to milk them in the early morning and taking their full bottles home.

(Courtesy of Shropshire Museum Service)

over 80%. Of those who survived, 65-85% were disfigured by scars, mainly on the face, whilst 5% suffered blindness. When an epidemic broke out in 1865 all the schools were immediately closed.[2] The disease was airborne and could be passed from an infected person to someone they lived with, came in contact with, or even via infected linen such as bedclothes. Because it was so infectious, when cases in adjoining counties were notified, such as in 1902, the local MOH was instructed by the council to spare no expense to ensure it was kept out of Ludlow. From such a parsimonious council as Ludlow's, this stresses the fear in which the disease was held.

When the annual May Fair arrived in that year, travellers' caravans were banned from the town except for those on the Smithfield, and the occupants of these had to undergo a medical inspection to ensure that they did not carry the disease.[3]

At the same time, Ludlow Council, in conjunction with the local Rural District Council, constructed an Isolation Hospital on the eastern side of the road leading from Rock Lane to the Sheet Road. This received its first patient in May 1903: a tramp travelling through the town and staying at a common lodging house in Holdgate Fee, who subsequently died. All lodging houses were immediately supplied with disinfectant. Two months later, occurred a second case when a man in a lodging house was diagnosed with smallpox. The property was disinfected immediately and all staying there were stopped from leaving and the council arranged for food to be sent in.[4]

The following year, two further patients were admitted to the Isolation Hospital, this time from the Casual Ward at the Workhouse on Gravel Hill. All bedding was burnt. Two years later, the hospital was required again for two children and their father. Sadly, though vaccinations were available, only 50% of local schoolchildren had been inoculated by

1912 due to parental misunderstandings and ill-founded fears. However, the threat of the disease diminished enough to allow the isolation hospital to be closed in 1933.[5]

Other Contagious Diseases

Scarlet fever, diphtheria and tuberculosis were three other infectious diseases that brought misery and fear to many families. They mainly affected children, with scarlet fever named after the colour of the skin rash that occurred, whilst diphtheria caused the neck to swell, blocking the airway and creating a barking cough. Both were very infectious, both airborne and both a major cause of death before the introduction of antibiotics.

Cases were frequent, with some years standing out. As regards scarlet fever, 1899 saw six cases, all children, and in six different households. 1912 saw eight cases in three households with the result that the MOH ordered the closure of the two schools that the children attended, an action that drew an unofficial censure from the council. It was claimed that it 'had caused a good deal of injury to the trade of the town' and 'had affected the Xmas trade by frightening away shoppers from Ludlow.' Scarlet fever was still prevalent at the start of the interwar years with thirteen cases in 1920.[6]

Diptheria was just as prevalent and it was a widespread outbreak of this disease in 1921 in conjunction with yet another outbreak of scarlet fever that forced the council to take notice and act against both diseases. A case of diphtheria was discovered at Ludlow's Cottage Hospital in College Street. Since isolation was the only known way of stopping the disease spreading, the hospital was closed for three weeks and all new patients turned away. The outbreak, however, was not confined. Cases appeared all over the town, many in homes where families lived in a just a few rooms and where

BUTCHERS – GRIFFITHS

Benjamin Griffiths had a butchers shop at 25 Bull Ring at the turn of the twentieth century with a slaughterhouse attached. As can be seen, in order to attract customers, meat was openly displayed outside the shop. This only ended in 1927 when the council finally passed a byelaw forcing butchers to install glass windows so that their meat was better protected from flies and wind-borne dirt.

(Courtesy of Ludlow Historical Research Group)

isolating an ill child was impossible. Such a difficulty was seen at 33 Rock Lane where a three-year-old child of a heavily pregnant mother died of diphtheria and a thirteen-month-old child also caught the disease. Finally, the ill infant was sent to an isolation hospital at Monksmoor, Shrewsbury, thirty miles away, as was another child from 'a poor home.' This had to be done because the Ministry of Health which controlled the smallpox isolation hospital in the town insisted that only those suffering from smallpox could be admitted. What concerned the council even more was that they would have to pay not only for transport for each patient but also for nursing care.

In 1921 a total of 88 cases of diphtheria were seen and, in addition, 66 cases of scarlet fever. The homes of the families concerned were fumigated with sulphur then lime-washed or repapered. In addition, schools were closed, as was the cinema. Worried by the growing cost as yet more children had to be transferred to Monksmoor hospital, the council decided that the cost to the rates was more than the town could afford

COTTAGE HOSPITAL

Situated on College Street until 1982 was the Cottage Hospital that had been opened thanks to an endowment by the Hon. Mary Windsor-Clive. Its stated purpose was for 'the relief of the industrious poor' of Ludlow but it was up to the trustees to decide on the definition of 'poor' and 'industrious.' Before the introduction of the National Health Service in 1948, anyone who fell outside the interpretation of these words was charged for treatment and this was a cause of much resentment at times.

(Courtesy of Shropshire Museum Service)

and stopped any more from going. This decision led to three operations having to be carried out by doctors in workmen's cottages, with two of the children dying. The ensuing outcry caused the council to think again.[7] Finally, the provision of a new isolation hospital for Ludlow, discussed many times before but always shelved, was now belatedly decided on.

Ludlow's New Isolation Hospital

It was built on land at the Smithfield which not many years before had been the local rubbish dump. Because of this, permission to build was only given after a public enquiry and, initially, for a maximum of three years, whilst another site was found. None was found and the original hospital remained as a permanent fixture. It opened on 5 January 1922 and was a converted army hut. The building had two wings, one reserved for scarlet fever patients and the other for those suffering from diphtheria. Staffed by two nurses, the two wards had separate entrances and could accommodate nine children in each. The centre of the building was split into sections: nurses' sitting room, nurses' bedroom, private ward for an adult, kitchen, drying room, and store room. For bathing, a wheeled bath was purchased that, after being filled with hot water, could be taken to wherever it was needed. Visiting was not allowed and mothers could only see their children through the windows.[8]

The hospital was certainly needed. In the year it opened the town suffered 46 cases of scarlet fever and 45 cases of diphtheria, and because of the difficulties of isolating patients in small, overcrowded cottages, 67 cases were admitted to the hospital in its first twelve months: 31 with scarlet fever and 36 with diphtheria. Its effectiveness was shown in that deaths from both diseases fell from fourteen children in 1921 to six in 1922. However, finance still dominated the thoughts of a number of councillors. Local authorities of patients from outside the borough were billed and consideration was given to charging local residents if it was thought that they could afford all or part of the costs of nursing.[9]

Tuberculosis

Notwithstanding the new isolation hospital, outbreaks of scarlet fever and diphtheria still remained common throughout the interwar years, as did tuberculosis. This latter airborne disease attacked the lungs and produced a chronic cough. The main cause was the milk supply. In 1922 it was estimated that up to 13% of all milk was infected with the tubercule bacilli. Pasteurisation was needed but Ludlow's local dairies were not equipped to do this. Until antibiotics were available and a vaccine developed, after the Second World War, there was no cure. The main treatment was good food, sunlight, fresh air and rest, all of which were virtually impossible for the working classes especially when they lived in the damp, overcrowded, ill-ventilated and dark courts and yards of Ludlow.[10]

Since the end of the nineteenth century, Ludlow's MOH had been calling for the testing of milk at all fifteen of the dairies which supplied the town but the small amount of testing that was introduced was intermittent at best. It was not helped when, even in the 1950s, children helped themselves to milk straight from the cow. Even though Ludlow children were 'townies', they were used to animals. For example, Brenda Oliver recalls that each evening, cows would be brought down the Linney and along Lower Corve Street to the dairy at the end of St Mary's Lane. Cattle, sheep and pigs were also walked through the town to the auction market near the railway station. Winifred Howard's mother always placed a board across the doorway of her house on Old Street, not just to keep her young children in but also to keep farm animals out. Brenda also remembers that, along with many other children, they went to visit the cows that were at the

HARP LANE

This is Harp Lane in the centre of Ludlow off Castle Square. In medieval times butchers solely populated it and even in the interwar years it was the site of at least one slaughterhouse. The effect on nearby residents and shoppers can be imagined. The Medical Officer of Health in 1922 commenting on another slaughterhouse in nearby Quality Square explained that 'the animals have to be driven down a narrow passage and I've no doubt cruelty results.' In addition 'flies in the summertime foul the meat.' Pigs were also kept at the slaughterhouse resulting in piles of manure being added to those of offal.

(Courtesy of Shropshire Museum Service)

auction yard overnight. *'We took a bottle up there and milked the cows. There was no sterilisation then.'* What was especially prized was the 'beastings'; the milk given by a cow that had just given birth to a calf [colostrum]. This was used to make an unusually rich custard or very soft sweetened cheese.

The annual MOH reports often blamed the state of housing in the borough as a major factor in the spread of tuberculosis and being detrimental to the treatment of it. In 1900 it was stated that:

'There is an undue proportion of cottages in this town which have neither back light or ventilation. This state of things is most conducive to the development of tubercular and general bad health and as long as this class of property is tolerated by the authorities, tuberculosis will tend to increase.'[11]

On visiting the homes of TB sufferers in 1912, the then MOH found himself making the same point:

'The lack of ventilation and lighting in several of the houses visited was marked and it was evident that little improvement in the condition of the patients could be expected at home.' In his view a sanatorium was needed.[12]

By the 1920s the council had acted on this latter advice and for tubercular patients in a serious condition, they did pay for them to attend the sanatorium at Prees Heath. However, the MOH was still stressing to the council that it was the poor housing that 'contributed very considerably to the high death rate and the high incidence of TB in the area.'[13] In the report for 1933, after fifteen new cases had been reported and four deaths from tuberculosis had occurred, the MOH once again told an apparently deaf council that *'the inadequate lighting and ventilation which is so frequent in the houses in the Courts is undoubtedly one of the causes of the high death rate from T.B.'*[14] At least a local TB After-Care Committee was set up which gave out free pasteurised milk to patients and their families and paid travel costs so that sufferers could be X-rayed. However, it was the county council rather than the borough council who financed this.[15]

Overall death rates, measured by how many deaths occurred per 1,000 inhabitants, though declining nationally from 1851-1901, were actually rising in Ludlow at the end of the nineteenth century. The local average death rate for the ten years 1880-1889 was 18.2 compared to 19.61 for the ten-year period 1895-1904. The MOH annual reports put this down, as they did with tuberculosis, to poor housing conditions. It was pointed out that in 1899 only eleven of the largest 33 towns in England and Wales had a higher death rate than Ludlow. Though the death rate then began falling, the rate of 14.6 in 1932 was still well above the national rate of 12.3. During the interwar years, the MOH was still putting the main blame on 'the large proportion of old houses in the old part of town which are much below the standard of healthy dwellings.'[16]

Slaughterhouses and Livestock

One other cause was the prevalence of unhealthy places such as slaughterhouses in close proximity to housing. Most butchers slaughtered animals either on their premises or nearby. There were eight such slaughterhouses in the centre of Ludlow at the beginning of the twentieth century. Complaints from those living nearby were common and had been voiced for years. In the 1860s, twelve local inhabitants wrote to the council:

'to call your attention to a great nuisance now existing in Quality Square and which consists of slaughterhouses and cesspools containing decomposed animal and vegetable matter, accumulated to such an extent as to be injurious to health, offensive to decency and prejudicial to the householders adjoining the locality.'

The Inspector of Nuisances who 'found a quantity of putrid fish and other very offensive matter supposed from

Health & Health Care

NAG'S HEAD YARD

This was the Nag's Head Yard entered by the side of the Nag's Head public house on Corve Street. This street had at least eight such courts and yards leading off it. Cheaply and quickly built in the late eighteenth and early nineteenth century these small cottages were often in a very poor state by 1900. With many being overcrowded, damp and having little natural light, the Medical Officer of Health constantly warned the council that they were a breeding ground for tuberculosis. Note the open drain running down the side of the yard back to the main street taking away not only domestic waste water but servicing the communal outside tap and wash-house.

(Courtesy of Lottie James)

a slaughterhouse thrown there' backed up this claim. The council asserted that nothing could be done at the moment whilst at the same time pointing out that a similar situation existed at a slaughterhouse at the back of the Narrows.[17]

Slaughterhouses were subject to annual inspection and after adverse reports by the MOH, members of the Sanitary Committee visited all eight of them in 1894 and 'found them in an extremely unsatisfactory condition.' Five had large, deep manure pits in which offal and other waste was deposited and common pit privies drained into two of them. As regards their emptying, byelaws were being broken at seven of them. This emptying was supposed to be done between the hours of 10pm and 6am but was often carried out during the day, with the offal being deposited in the street to await the cart to take it away. Prosecutions were rare.[18]

It appears that nothing had changed by the end of the First World War when complaints were still being made

WATKINS THE BUTCHERS – TOWER STREET

Up until the Second World War butchers in Ludlow were supplied by slaughterhouses in the centre of the town often owned by the individual butchers themselves. In the nineteenth century, this butchers shop at 5 Tower Street killed its animals just behind the premises though by the 1920s, when this photograph was taken, the slaughterhouse had moved to Corve Street. As regards hygiene, however, little had changed. The Medical Officer of Health in 1926 complained that 'pigs are here kept in close proximity to the slaughterhouse and are, together with the manure, a serious damage to the meat.'

(Courtesy of Shropshire Museum Service)

regarding the stench from both the waste and the boiling of offal in town centre slaughterhouses. In 1925 the MOH again reported to the council on the health issues such places posed. The one in Quality Square, then owned by a butcher with premises on the High Street, was still causing worries.

'The entrance to these premises is very hard, the animals have to be driven down a narrow passage and I've no doubt cruelty results. ... Flies in the summertime foul the meat and spoils (sic) its keeping qualities.'[19]

The council ignored the recommendation of the MOH that all slaughterhouses should be closed and a public abattoir

Health & Health Care

built on the outskirts of town. Slaughterhouses remained in the centre of Ludlow until the Government forced their closure during the Second World War and built an abattoir at Craven Arms, in order to carry out meat rationing more efficiently.

One other health issue, constantly highlighted by successive MOHs, was that of the keeping of pigs in the cramped Yards and Courts. Throughout the second half of the 19th century, the Inspector of Nuisances was inundated with complaints regarding problems with piles of manure together with the stench of blood when the animals were killed. At 143 Corve Street, after pigs were slaughtered, it was claimed that blood ran down the passage and across the pavement. Also in Corve Street, at the top of the Spread Eagle Yard *'pig wash and other offensive matter (was stored) in tubs so as to be a*

CORVE STREET AND HORSE DROPPINGS

This c.1865 view up Corve Street highlights one other nineteenth century health hazard: that of animal dung. Not only were roads and footpaths soiled by cows being taken for their daily milking but also by cattle, sheep and pigs being walked to market. In addition, all transport was horse pulled with the result that horse droppings were a constant sight on all roads as this photograph attests. Crossing the road without soiling their skirts was next to impossible for Victorian ladies and certainly impossible as regards footwear for everyone.

(Courtesy of Shropshire Museum Service)

nuisance to the neighbours.' At Badger's Yard, Lower Galdeford, pig manure swamped the court whilst at No. 84 pigs were kept just one yard from the back door. Similar complaints were made about the foul state of piggeries close to a number of cottages in Lower Broad Street. The MOH confirmed that such practices were still common in the yards and courts in the first half of the twentieth century. The keeping of pigs was also carried on at the slaughterhouses. Ten were being kept in Quality Square in 1894 and little had changed by 1925 when the MOH reported pigs being kept in sties at six town-centre slaughterhouses close to where meat was being cut.[20] As will be seen in Chapter 6, pig rearing and slaughtering by householders was still prevalent in the 1950s.

Infant Mortality

However, the main aspect of health that worried a number of MOH over the years was the number of babies that died at birth and the Borough's infant mortality rate. In the nineteenth century nearly all babies born in Ludlow were born at home and, for the working classes, this continued until the National Health Service was set up in 1948. There were a few exceptions. A woman having an illegitimate child, who had nobody to care for her, could have her child in the workhouse infirmary, but this was avoided if at all possible because of the attached stigma.

    A charity was set up in 1810 named the Society for the Relief of Lying-In Women. It was run by a committee of twelve ladies and supported by gifts and subscriptions. In return, each subscriber was allowed to recommend one woman annually but all had to be 'married women of good reputation.' Each of the favoured women was given sheets, a bed-gown and cap, flannels, napkins and other necessary articles. All had to be returned after five weeks. By 1869 three doctors were giving their time free of charge, and some maternity clothes were also now being loaned out. A few 'necessitous cases' were even given a small amount of cash. All still had to be recommended and be respectable. The charity was still in operation in 1932 and retained the part-time services of two qualified midwives 'who attended at a very moderate charge, the wives of those who are unable to afford a higher fee.'[21]

But for the majority of working class wives there was no such help. The delivery of a baby was usually left to a local woman who was called in on such occasions and was then given a small payment. Such women were often also the ones who acted as a nurse when one was required and even washed and laid out the dead. Almost certainly they also helped women with miscarriages and abortions. Even after the law made it illegal from 1902 to practise as a midwife unless trained, such women were still used at births since they were not only cheaper but were known and trusted by the mothers. One such woman was Charlotte French, the grandmother of Daphne French. During the interwar years, Charlotte acted as midwife and laid out the dead for Lower Broad Street, having a different apron for each task. In Holdgate Fee, Freda

CORVE DAIRY

Milk production was local and in 1907 there were twelve dairies, cowsheds and milk-shops in Ludlow. Up until the mid-twentieth century milk was still often delivered to homes in churns and ladled out to housewives. This led the local Medical Officers of Health to constantly warn the council of the link between unpasteurized milk and tuberculosis. Corve Milk Dairy, owned by T.H. Davies, was still in business in 1960.

(Courtesy of Shropshire Museum Service)

Stewart recalls her mother helping out the 'street midwife' when a neighbour was in labour, on a number of occasions. On Sandpits Avenue, Sheila Burmingham remembers that it was an Ethel Glaze who laid out the dead and, prior to the advent of the National Health Service, often acted as midwife. Nationally 65% of all births in 1937 were still taking place at home and there is no reason to believe this was not at least the case in Ludlow where it was probably much higher.[22]

Having a child at home sometimes brought with it problems. A number of families, such as that of Joan Thomas, could only afford one set of sheets. This meant that they would

FARM – ST MARY'S LANE

Until the last quarter of the twentieth century farms could still be found within the borough boundary. One was in St Mary's Lane. As can be seen by the trail of cattle dung in this photograph of 1962, cows were daily herded along the Linney, down Corve Street and then turned into the lane to the farm for milking. Every morning they would return the same way to their fields. The wall and farm building on the left have now been demolished to give access to the housing development of St Mary's Mews.

(Courtesy of Shropshire Museum Service)

have to be washed, dried, ironed and replaced all on the same day. When her mother gave birth, a close friend or relation stepped in to replace the soiled bed linen. As a result 'they had a nice pair of sheets and no-one knew they had none.'

The local statistics for stillbirths or death within minutes or hours of birth was a continuing concern for the MOH especially given the poor state of the cottages in which most were being born. Even as late as the 1940s the then – MOH was highlighting that the eight stillbirths that occurred in Ludlow in 1946 was twice the national average. A major factor in these figures was the high illegitimacy rate. In the ten years 1902-11 the average percentage of all births in the borough that were illegitimate was 9.8% but could reach 15%, as it did in 1911. The figure remained high in the inter-war years with the rate in 1921 being 11.5% and it was mainly these children who did not survive. Of the eleven babies who died that year, six were illegitimate: over 50%.[23]

Giving birth to a child whilst unmarried was a social stigma for both the mother-to-be and her family. Consequently, hiding such a pregnancy was common but the result was often fatal, whether intentionally or unintentionally, and the local newspapers often carried such sad stories. In 1857 a newly-born child was strangled, wrapped in an apron and thrown off a cliff behind the Charlton Arms Inn. Meant for the river, it was discovered by a boy playing on the bank. In 1862 a newly-born baby was found in the river near Corve Bridge. It appeared that it had been born without medical care and had died from a blow to the side of the head. 1872 witnessed a baby found wrapped in a linen and paper parcel in a culvert at Steventon whilst in 1892, at the bottom of Lower Mill Street, a playing child found a body of a stillborn baby girl in the river. Infanticide reared its head yet again a year later when a Sarah James was committed to Shrewsbury for the murder of her newly-born illegitimate baby boy.

The first years of the twentieth century saw such tragedies continue. Another young mother, Ellen Everall, alongside her mother, was charged with concealing a birth and manslaughter in 1904 when her newly-born child was found sewn up in an old bodice in the River Teme.[24]

Little had seemingly changed by the interwar years. The hiding of such pregnancies until the last moment, due to the social shame attached, was still leading to tragedies. The newly born child of a deserted wife living on New Road was found laid out in a suitcase by the bed. It was felt that it would have survived if medical attention had been called. It was the same for an unmarried domestic servant at Castle Lodge. When the maternity nurse arrived, called by the maid's employers, she found the mother fully dressed and the baby on the floor dying from accidental damage to the head. The extent of illegitimacy locally can be judged by the fact that the Ludlow Archdeaconry employed a social worker to help single girls who were known to be pregnant. In the year ending June 1934 she dealt with 42 such pregnancies with the average age of most mothers being eighteen and the youngest fifteen.[25]

As for the infant mortality rate, this was measured by the number of infants who died before the age of twelve months per 1,000 births. Nationally the rate fell from 1851 but Ludlow's, as well as being consistently above the national rate, actually increased. In the 1890s when nationally the figure was just over 140 that of Ludlow reached 160.4 in 1898. Though the rate fell back to 137 deaths per thousand in 1906, it was still far higher than the national figure of just over 110. The seriousness of the situation in Ludlow can be seen in that the national rate was also the average for all the rest of urban Shropshire, whilst in the rural sections of the county the rate was just 85. The cause of these high figures was, in part, poor and overcrowded housing but also ignorance of child welfare,

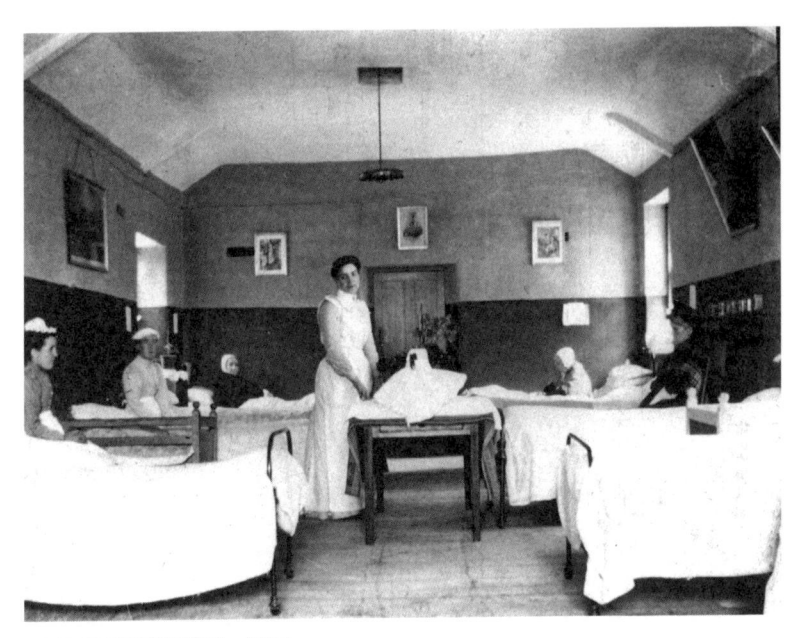

WARD AT WORKHOUSE c.1920

By 1920 most of the inmates at the workhouse on Gravel Hill were the old and infirm who could no longer look after themselves at home and had no family to support them. Though this posed picture appears to show that they were well looked after the real situation was highlighted by the local Medical Officer of Health in 1937 when he reported that walls were damp, there was no hot or cold water in any of the wards and the inmates had to cross 30 yards of open space in all weathers to reach the lavatories. (Courtesy of Shropshire Museum Service)

especially as regards the feeding of infants. In 1900 the MOH felt compelled to issue to young mothers a card giving helpful advice as what to do and what not to do. The MOH was still highlighting the dangers of not feeding babies properly in 1947. Of the seven babies who died that year, three of the deaths were due to gastroenteritis and, it was claimed, 'these could probably have been prevented by proper care of the children's diet and a higher standard of domestic hygiene.' Sheila Stephens recalls that when her prematurely-born brother was born at home during the Second World War, weighing just 2½lbs, the local grocer gave her mother 'condensed milk

**WOMAN AND CHILDREN
OUTSIDE A LUDLOW COTTAGE**

This posed picture, almost certainly taken c.1860 by an amateur photographer whose interest was caught by the attractive yet dilapidated cottage porch, shows two main points of interest. The first is the poverty that can be seen etched on the faces of the children and especially the young girl. Secondly, the woman, who is almost certainly the mother, shows how the strain of keeping a family on a limited income, allied to the daily drudgery of hard, physical housework that took its toll on health, brought about premature aging. (Courtesy of Shropshire Archives) as a special favour to feed him.' As for housing conditions, the death of an eight-week-old baby in a cottage in the Red Lion Yard off Raven Lane highlighted the danger to young infants when sleeping space was at a premium. This infant, who had to sleep in the same bed as its mother and eight-year-old brother, was found suffocated in the morning. Such tragedies were not uncommon. Similar deaths were occurring in overcrowded cottages even after the Second World War. In St John's Road, a mother's sister and her family were staying until they could find a house of their own and this meant that some of the children had to sleep in their parents' bed. As a result a young baby suffocated.[26]

However, Ludlow did see the infant mortality rate fall quite dramatically from the early 1920s. The turning point was the opening of a Child Welfare Centre in Corve Street in 1921. This was not due to the generosity of the borough council since it was the Ministry of Health and Shropshire County Council who each supplied 50% of the costs. At first it was only open one day a week to both expectant and new mothers but by the end of the first year, 110 names were on the register. Baby clothes were provided by the Red Cross and sold or given to new mothers. Also sold at cost price, or given free to those whose husbands were unemployed, were milk foods, cod liver oil and cleansing cream.

In 1923 the centre moved to Dinham. Maternity bags were now 'lent to the very poor cases,' health and child welfare talks given three times a month and classes were held to teach young mothers how to make clothes for the under-fives. Services continued to be added. Schoolchildren could attend for medical examination on Monday or Saturday mornings, and this service soon expanded with the centre becoming the home of a school clinic. In addition, orthopaedic aftercare nurses were given a room every Monday. This service grew so popular that when the orthopaedic nurses were present 'the

Centre is so crowded that the patients overflow into the passages and garden.' By 1929 this Child Welfare Clinic, which now catered for both Ludlow and the outlying area, had 747 pre-school children on the books. Free-milk tickets were given to mothers with infants or 'delicate' children under three years, and young mothers and their children could receive free dental treatment from a dentist who came once every six months for two weeks at a time. Shortly after, ill babies were sent, at the County Council's cost, to the Home for Ailing Babies in Wellington for treatment. Even though this removal from the mother, often for many weeks, must have been keenly felt, it was claimed by the middle-class managers of the centre that:

'This is much appreciated by the mothers who cannot possibly look after these ailing infants properly in their own homes. The infants return bonny after a few months.'

By the 1930s an after-care service had also been introduced. Children below the age of one year received at least six home visits from a nurse during those first twelve months.[27]

The result was dramatic. Within a year of the Welfare Centre opening, the infant mortality rate for the borough had halved and by 1928 it was 25, the lowest ever recorded in the town and compared to an average of 69 for England and Wales. It carried on falling and though it rose to match the national average in 1933, due to a rise in poverty caused by high unemployment, the rate soon fell again.

The Health of Housewives

The health of housewives was also far from good but mainly unremarked on at the time. Their general poor health, caused by long hours of housework, carried on often when pregnant time and time again, appears to have been taken for granted. This was highlighted when a national study into the health of housewives was carried out in the 1930s in which 1,250 women, aged between 20 and 50, and living in cities, towns and villages, were surveyed.[28] 31% of the group believed that they were in relatively good health though given the ailments that they said they suffered from it was felt that, if examined by a doctor, they would have been put in a different category. 23% said they had indifferent health meaning that they listed one or more ailments of a chronic nature. 15% felt that they suffered from bad health, which meant that they listed ailments that were both numerous and serious, whilst the remaining 31% classed themselves as in very bad health. This meant that they suffered from a number of serious, chronic conditions. 558 women said they were anaemic; 291 had recurring headaches; 273 were constipated both with and without haemorrhoids;

QUALITY SQUARE

For many years Quality Square, being the site of an abattoir, pigsties and a cesspit, was continually being criticised by the local Medical Officer of Health. It still housed the abattoir of Babbage's the High Street butchers in the interwar years. By 1960, as this photograph shows, the square was in dire need of improvement and this warehouse, owned by Price's the plumbers and next door to Price's the bakers (now Ego's), was soon to be demolished.

(Courtesy of Ludlow Historical Research Group)

191 had various gynaecological problems, though based on the symptoms described, a further 203 could be added to this figure; 165 had constant toothache; and 101 suffered from varicose veins, ulcerated or white legs etc. Other ailments included backache, neuritis and neuralgia, bladder and gastric problems, cystitis, gallstones, respiratory disorders, asthma, bronchitis, indigestion, and so the list went on.

In such health these women had to carry out the household chores.

Daily Life of a Ludlow Housewife

The average daily life of working-class women, and of most wives and mothers in Ludlow, followed a common pattern. Many spent a sleepless night, often having a child in the bedroom and sometimes having to feed a baby during the night. They arose at about 6.30am to stoke up the cooking-range fire, fetch water and heat it for a cup of tea and personal washing whilst cooking breakfast for their husbands and elder children if they too went to work. Then they had to prepare packed lunches for them before waking the younger children and feeding them before they went off to school.

They would often have their own breakfasts whilst on their feet doing these chores. Then there was the house to clean, washing up to be done, beds to be made, and food prepared for the children when they came home at midday. It has to be remembered that there were few amenities for cooking, limited cookware and few utensils. In addition, since there was nowhere to store food, a daily trip to the shops had to be made. An evening meal then had to be prepared for the family and hot water ready if their husbands needed to wash. Once again the wives often ate after all the rest and whilst on their feet. After getting the children to bed, it could be eight o'clock. They could then sit down but there would always be sewing, mending and knitting to be done. Washdays brought strenuous additional chores to be fitted in as described in Chapter 3, and on wet days clothes would have to be dried in front of the fire range on which they cooked. To make everything more tiring all this would often have to be done whilst pregnant, as large families were the norm for many. Nursing of sick children or even a sick husband could just add to the daily burden and, in the latter case, on less money. On Sundays all this had to be done with all the family squashed into perhaps just one downstairs room and a small scullery.

The Health of Ludlow's Working Class Men in 1914

As regards the health of the male population of Ludlow, viewing the surviving medical reports of those who joined the armed forces in World War One can open a window. Albeit that they are relatively cursory in content, they are still illuminating. Of the 92 surviving records studied, 85 appear to be men from a working-class background. Their average height was 5ft 6ins, average weight nine stone and average unexpanded chest measurement 33'. This compares with the seven records of men from middle-class families who had an average height of 5ft 8½ins. The weight of only two of these men was recorded but both were over 10½ stone. The difference is quite startling.

It is also interesting to note that the only record of a working-class man after his initial twelve weeks training records him having put on 5lbs in weight and adding an extra inch to his chest. This must have been the result of a regular diet rather than physical fitness since he had been a labourer in civilian life. One other fact that stands out is that the most common medical defect listed was that of bad teeth, the result of not being able to afford dental treatment.[29]

Healthcare

Healthcare for those with little money was always difficult. Doctors and dentists both wanted payment for their services. Until 1874, for most of the working classes in Ludlow, their only choice was asking for medical help from the Poor Law Guardians or from a charitable dispensary.

As part of outdoor relief dispensed by the Poor Law Guardians, the poor who were ill could ask to see the District Medical Officer who could then recommend such patients to be allowed food and drink to build up their strength, or some form of medicine. It is telling that of the first 74 applicants for out relief in 1860/61, 54 were recommended by the medical officer. This emphasises the fact that many local families could just keep out of abject poverty until a doctor's bill needed paying, or the breadwinner became ill.

By the 1890s, the sick, and especially the aged poor, could receive items in addition to the usual bread and mutton such as milk and even be visited by a nurse.[30]

The alternative place in 1851 for the poor to turn to for medical help was the Ludlow Charitable Dispensary. Founded in 1835 for the relief of the sick poor, it was originally in Castle Street but soon moved to 56 Broad Street. Philanthropic subscribers were given two tickets to hand out to deserving cases for every ½ guinea they subscribed.

The dispensary's opening hours were 10-11 each morning and 5-6 each evening and patients had to bring with them their own receptacles to hold any medicine prescribed. Considering that Ludlow was home to over 4,000 people, the numbers helped were not great, with just 241 cases seen throughout the whole of 1891 and this appears to have been the norm.

The charity was still giving out medicine in 1917 though it appears to have closed down during the 1920s.[31]

The Ladies Benevolent Fund, a charity set up to assist the sick and needy, gave further help. In 1868 they gave out tickets to the families of 619 sick patients to be exchanged for items such as meat, bread, groceries and wine. Still going strong in 1888, their aid was given on the recommendation of thirty ladies of the Ludlow Church of England District Visiting Society who ventured into the numerous courts and yards of Ludlow visiting families said to be in need. The Benevolent Fund also kept a stock of sheets and other linen that could be loaned out to those who suffered illness.[32]

The town's sick were next helped with the opening of the Cottage Hospital in 1874. Mary Windsor-Clive, who died in 1873, left in her will £7,000 in trust for 'the poor sick of Ludlow.' The next year a building was purchased in College Street and fitted out. In addition to the money in the trust fund, local people could become subscribers and the trustees also organised money-raising activities. Throughout the remainder of the nineteenth century and the first quarter of the twentieth, the average number of in-patients admitted was one hundred. The small operating theatre saw about one operation a week and in the early 1930s X-ray equipment was installed.

In addition to such medical care an Outdoor Relief Fund ensured that patients also received aftercare and, on the recommendation of one of the doctors who were linked to the hospital, fifty or sixty families were visited and nursed in their own homes. Milk was distributed, as were hot dinners or pints of broth or soup and body strengthening brandy, port and whisky. Blankets, sheets, nightgowns and other sick room necessities were loaned out in addition to items such as crutches.[33]

Considering the population of the town, the number of sick helped was relatively small and certainly less than the capacity of which the hospital was capable. One reason for this came to light in a public debate in 1934. The Rector of St Laurence's Church, who was on the board of trustees, believed that:

> 'There was still a feeling amongst certain sections of the parish that admission to Ludlow Cottage Hospital was a difficult and expensive matter, and that it was easier for patients to be sent to Shrewsbury, Hereford or Birmingham.'

Defining Poor

He pointed out that the hospital existed for the free nursing of the poor of Ludlow and no admission ticket was necessary, just the recommendation of one of the five doctors who serviced the hospital. This elicited a reply from a 'working man' who asked how 'the poor of Ludlow' were defined? Are you 'poor' if you are in receipt of a wage: and what was actually being offered free: was it just treatment or maintenance such as food? The Rector did not answer directly but quoted the original trust deed that said the hospital was 'for the relief of the industrious poor who are not habitual recipients of relief under the Poor Law Act.' In other words 'the deserving poor.' It was up to the trustees to decide who were deserving and they also took into consideration the total family income and the size of the family, to decide if the patient should be asked to pay part or all of the costs or none at all.

That many had been asked to pay is shown in the Hospital's annual report for 1931/32. This highlighted the fact that due to high unemployment in the town, payments received from patients had fallen by £74.[34] Because of possible costs, many preferred to use the services of unofficial 'wise women'. A number of the residents of Lower Broad Street chose to consult Beatrice Nash who lived among them. Daphne French's aunt had her broken arm set by her whilst Beatrice also supplied homemade poultices for cuts.

Health Insurance 1932-48

The more serious of Ludlow's sick were often now choosing to go to the Voluntary Hospitals, and the one at Shrewsbury in particular. These too were charitable institutions but were preferred as they offered a cheap insurance scheme. This was introduced in Ludlow in 1932 for all those who earned under £420 p.a. and volunteers went door-to-door asking people to sign up to paying 1d or 2d a week towards the upkeep of the Royal Salop Infirmary. In return, after paying a subscription for eight weeks, they were entitled to free nursing and maintenance at any of the Shropshire Voluntary Hospitals. (This excluded the Ludlow Cottage Hospital.) By 1946 the weekly cost had risen to 4d per week for a man over 21, 3d for a woman over 16 years and the same for young men aged 16-21. However, if the man was married, his wife and any children up to the school-leaving age were also covered. The scheme ended with the birth of the National Health Service in July 1948.[35]

Ludlow's Workhouse Infirmary

The only other institution offering health care was the old workhouse at Gravel Hill. In 1929, under an Act of Parliament, this was removed from the control of the Poor Law Guardians and was handed over to the local authority. The infirmary section then mainly looked after the aged infirm. The MOH, however, gave the conditions there a damning report in 1937. Though the infirmary had room for sixty patients, it held at that time just 23 men, ten women and four children. Of these, ten were permanently bedridden and twenty so old that they needed constant nursing care. Looking after them were just three nurses during the day, one temporary night nurse, and a charwoman. The MOH believed a minimum of six nurses were needed along with further temporary nurses during the winter months. He branded much of the equipment as 'disgraceful.' It was either in short supply or damaged. For example, there were only four screens for the sixty beds. Many walls were damp, and hot and cold water was not provided on the wards. The buildings also housed the elderly who could no longer look after themselves in their own homes. Even they had to cross thirty yards of open yard in all weathers to reach a lavatory.[36]

Once the National Health Service came into existence in 1948 the old workhouse became the East Hamlet Hospital and came under the control of the Local Hospitals Management Committee which visited it in early 1949. It too was shocked, especially at the plight of the elderly inmates.

'Men and women are housed in separate buildings erected over one hundred years ago. Each has one long common room with cold stone floors and one fireplace around which all huddle on cold days. The rooms have low ceilings with dull, drab walls unable to take paint because of the plaster rotting with age. There is no privacy even in the sleeping quarters which are long dormitories. Residents include patients suffering from senility and mental trouble.'

Yet another committee member was moved to exclaim:

'I was so appalled at the conditions I saw there that I was ashamed of being a Salop County Councillor. Inmates were huddled together in conditions that could only be described as extremely bad, and on the faces of some of these poor old folk there was no ray of hope.'

Even worse, it was found that the residents still had to work for their keep.[37]

NHS in Ludlow

Improvements at last began to be implemented and purpose-built old-people's homes were recommended for construction with just the hospital remaining on the site of the old workhouse. Dignity for Ludlow's aged poor was at last on the agenda.

The Cottage Hospital also saw rapid change under the new Health Service. Within a year, eight consultants were available, and in a six-month period 162 theatre operations were carried out, 217 X-rays taken and 228 patients admitted.[38]

With the coming of the National Health Service, medical provision for the bulk of the population of Ludlow changed dramatically. Doctors could be consulted free of charge, prescribed medicines collected from the chemists, and the cost of hospital treatment became just a memory. In addition, for the first time, working-class families could have dental work carried out. Many still lived in unhealthy, dark and damp houses, but at least the illnesses brought on by such poor living conditions could now be treated.

CHAPTER SIX

Life on the Edge of Poverty

Ludlow had a low-wage economy. As was seen in Chapter 1, after the decline of the glove industry during the first half of the nineteenth century, Ludlow returned to being a market town serving rural south Shropshire. This meant that in addition to jobs in building, quarrying and the railway, most employment was either in agriculture or serving agriculture, and this industry had always been a low-paid section of the economy.

Seasonal unemployment was also a problem for many families. Not being based indoors, most local employment was dependent upon the weather and in winter especially, many men found themselves laid off with no pay. During the harsh winter of 1894/95 an editorial in the *Ludlow Advertiser* pointed out how the poor weather conditions affected the families of many workers.

'The long continued severe weather, putting as it does a stop to nearly all outdoor work, is causing an amount of poverty and suffering greater than has been experienced for many years past.'[1]

Winter had always been the main period of distress for Ludlow's poor. In November 1866, the local coroner censured the relieving officer of the workhouse for refusing to take Elizabeth Beddoes of Lower Galdeford into his institution. As a result her two infant children died of starvation.[2]

At the turn of the twentieth century a fellow worker

who had an indoor job pleaded for help for those outside workers who had been laid off. He made an:

'appeal on behalf of the poor women and children of our town who, during the winter have suffered severely from the lack of employment by the breadwinner of the family, who must now in the present severe weather be reduced to the verge of starvation. I feel sure there are in Ludlow many ladies and gentlemen who would do something for the poor children who need food, or the poor mother who hears her babe crying for that sustenance which, owing to want and through no fault of her own, she cannot give.'[3]

Fifty years later in 1947, winter weather was still causing widespread distress. Many of the 300 men on the unemployment register were in the building trade and had been laid off, being unable to carry on their work in the cold conditions.[4]

The Unemployed

Unemployment, of course, was not just seasonal and at times when an industry such as agriculture went into decline or the national economy went into recession, Ludlow was not spared. The economic downturn following the First World War was felt here. Unemployment pay was still in its infancy. The *National Insurance Act of 1911* covered 2.3 million workers though not their dependents and was for only 15 weeks in any one year. The Act of 1920 extended unemployment benefit to nearly all workers though was still limited to just fifteen weeks. As a result, in Ludlow in November 1921 it was estimated that about one hundred men, many of whom had just returned from years in the trenches, were receiving the weekly 'dole' of 15/- but that scores more were either not eligible or no longer received it as they had come to the end of their time limit. One wife wrote pleading for help for her husband and many others like him who daily congregated at the Buttercross. He had had only one month's work in the last twelve.[5]

AFTERNOON TEA – BROAD STREET

In 1901, a genteel tea is taken in the rear garden of Elizabeth Hope's house in Broad Street. A lady of independent means, she entertains friends including the De Peele family of Church House, Ashford Bowdler. Such a scene epitomises the gulf that existed between the classes in Ludlow at this time. Not many yards away in Lower Broad Street and Frog Lane (St John's Road) other families struggled in poverty.
(Courtesy of Shropshire Museum Service)

High unemployment in the town lasted throughout the 1920s. In January 1926, 303 workers were looking for work and the figure was virtually unchanged a year later at 297. In addition, 43 others, mainly working at the Clee Hill Quarry, were on short time. The Secretary of the Shropshire Unemployment Committee held out 'little prospect of any great improvement. For a town of the size of Ludlow, the position was serious.' By 1929 the situation had improved only very slightly, with 234 workers without jobs, but then came the Wall Street Crash in the USA and worldwide economic recession. Even in the spring of 1931/32, when fresh seasonal work should have brought more job opportunities, the number unemployed reached 353 and in January 1933 the Chamber of Commerce estimated that one in four households in the town was affected by unemployment. It was only the outbreak of war in 1939 that remedied the problem.[6] By then, many Ludlow families had faced two decades of struggle.

Poor Relief Fund

One way that the families of the unemployed were helped began in the mid-nineteenth century when money was collected from the better-off sections of society and used to subsidise the sale of coal, rice, bread and soup to those in need. In 1847 alone 3,000 gallons of soup and 8,100 loaves of bread were supplied to Ludlow's needy poor.[7] This help was then set on a more permanent footing when it became the norm for the mayor of the town to set up a Poor Relief Fund each winter to which most middle-class residents subscribed.

BOYS SWIMMING IN RIVER TEME
With many families living in small, overcrowded cottages in cramped yards and courts, the natural playground for children was the streets or the surrounding countryside and especially the banks of the River Teme. These boys are almost certainly pupils of the Grammar School who took their swimming lessons above the Mill Street weir. Most working class boys would not have had swimming costumes and swam in their underpants or 'in a state of nature.' Complaints that this was causing embarrassment to ladies walking along the Bread Walk were being constantly voiced in the council chamber. (Courtesy of Shropshire Museum Service)

A committee, on which, among others, sat the mayor, fellow councillors and the Rector of St Laurence's Church, then organised a soup kitchen and the distribution of tickets that could be exchanged for food and coal. The Headmaster's log for 1864 at the boys' section of the National School, situated in Lower Galdeford, notes that several boys were absent on 19 January to help take home the coal that was being distributed to the poor. Similar absences were seen two days later when soup was served out to families in need. The log in the girls' section showed the same.

In January 1870, 800 gallons of soup was ladled out to the poor and in 1894 soup was still being provided for the many families suffering from a lack of work during the winter months. Four times 500-600 quarts of hot soup was made and given out at the Market Hall and four times, tickets, to be exchanged for food and coal, were given to those in need.

In the following winter, the distress in the town was so great that though once again four ticket distributions were made, the mayor, out of his own pocket, paid for a further twenty tons of coal. He then pleaded for those who could to donate more to do so for the 'especially needy', and Marston's Bros gave a loaf of bread to all those that received a coal ticket. The soup kitchen also now opened twice in a week again serving 550 quarts each time but it was still not enough to satisfy the people's hunger.[8]

This annual attempt to alleviate distress continued into the twentieth century. Seven ticket distributions for both food and coal were made from the council chamber in the winter of 1923/4 and, in 1929, 1,811 tickets to be exchanged for necessities were given to suffering families. By the winter of 1931/32 the need for help had risen to such an extent that, in addition to the usual subscriptions, funds had to be topped up with the proceeds from a number of concerts and other fund-raising activities. Unsurprisingly, middle-class worries

Life on the Edge of Poverty 121

THE BUTTERCROSS AND UNEMPLOYED MEN
Over the years unemployed men often gathered at the Buttercross as they waited for a job opportunity to arrive. Many jobs in Ludlow were casual ones. Workers were taken on for specific tasks and then laid off until fresh work was available, or were in outside work that could not be done when weather was bad. Winter was especially a time of high unemployment in the town often necessitating the opening of charitable, communal soup kitchens. (Courtesy of Shropshire Museum Service)

that 'scroungers' were abusing this charitable work began, not for the first time, to be aired, with one gentleman, who was helping to serve the soup, being said to have remarked that he had filled the same bowl three times. Despite such claims, in the winter of 1932/33 Mayor William Parsonage decided that the children of the 200-300 unemployed men of the town needed extra help and opened up a soup kitchen just for them at the Salvation Army Citadel in Lower Galdeford. He requested gifts not only of money but also of vegetables, meat or bones. In February the kitchen opened and over 200 quarts of soup were served to children three times a week at lunchtime. Very soon the elderly poor were also being served, so great was the hardship felt.[9]

Attempts to ensure that the children of the poor received at least one hot meal during the winter weeks had been tried earlier. The plight of families with young children suffering from the lack of a wage entering the household touched the conscience of the editor of the *Ludlow Advertiser* in 1921. He spoke of 'a good deal of distress borne in silence in the town' and of children especially who were 'suffering from a lack of sufficient nourishing food.' The newspaper opened up a shilling fund to pay for a breakfast kitchen using the facilities at the Salvation Army Citadel. From 8am children sat down with their bowls and spoons that they had brought with

THE GLOBE

The occasion for this photograph, taken outside the Globe public house in Market Street, is the celebration of Queen Victoria's Diamond Jubilee in 1897. What can also be discerned from the dress and faces of many in this crowd of regulars and passers by is the daily hardship they faced.

(Courtesy of Shropshire Museum Service)

them to eat their pint of soup or porridge along with bread and jam. Meals were served seven days a week and 2,200 were consumed in the first five weeks. The same service was offered the following year, though the charity had to move to the Harp Room in Church Street due to the new Salvation Army officer in charge listening to complaints that those attending religious services had had their clothes stained with globules of food that had not been cleaned up properly. The newspaper editor was not pleased with this uncharitable decision and complained that:

'the majority of children who came for their breakfasts will (now) have to trudge through rain and snow to a less central place situated further away from all three schools rather than the Citadel in Galdeford.'

However, no doubt with conscience salved, his newspaper soon stopped providing such breakfasts and the £26 left over, and discovered later in a dormant bank account, was used to purchase shoes for those children felt most in need.[10]

A number of individuals and organisations, including the churches, also arranged to give one-off meals for the poor during hard winters. In January 1885, 160 of the 'deserving poor' sat down to boiled beef, bread and butter, and cake and tea at the Congregational Chapel in Old Street. 120 children of the poor were given a dinner of soup and bread followed by plum pudding at the Wesleyan Sunday School in 1895, whilst the aged poor were treated to a ham and cakes tea at the Salvation Army Citadel in January 1899. This became an annual event, with food supplied by local tradesmen, and was still happening in 1929.[11] In 1933 the British Legion's Women's Committee and the Townswomen's Guild organised a Christmas meal for 450 children of the poor, following it up with another a year later, with boys from the Grammar School arriving to sing carols. At the third, now annual, meal, over 500 attended and:

'Long before the appointed hour, long strings of children waited outside the Town Hall and within a short time of the opening of the doors, every seat was filled and some children were standing by waiting for a vacancy…Of the tea itself, suffice it to say that little or nothing was left within a few minutes.'[12]

Each year Councillor Shinton and his wife treated poor pensioners to a Christmas meal, the seventh such being in 1945. Held at De Greys in Broad Street, the chosen old folk, clutching their entry ticket, sat at two lines of tables that stretched the entire length of the café and were served with roast chicken and vegetables followed by Christmas pudding, beer or tea.[13] But, though undoubtedly welcome, such isolated charitable offerings did little to alleviate the daily grind of poverty felt by many in Ludlow.

Temporary Work for the Unemployed

The town council, in an attempt to ensure more lasting help, periodically provided the unemployed with temporary work. In 1850 thirty unemployed men were set to work constructing a new path on the Whitcliffe. Such men could also be given stones to break, a task that vagrants calling in at the workhouse were required to do for their keep. In return, the men were paid in cash or sometimes in kind, usually with tickets that could be exchanged for bread or other staple foods. This carried on in the twentieth century. In 1922 the council had 200 tons of rough stone dumped on the Smithfield and paid the unemployed to break it. This was repeated in the next year and the following one when 400 tons was delivered to the Smithfield.

The unemployed were also given other work. When heavy snowfall occurred, they would be paid to clear the roads. Again, this began in the nineteenth century. Eighty men were employed to clear the streets in 1895 and for working from

Life on the Edge of Poverty

5am to 10.30am they received 1/6d. It was remarked at the time that for men to turn out to earn such a small amount for 5½ hours of hard labour showed how much in need they were. In 1933 one hundred men were taken on to clear drifts of up to 15ft in Rock Lane whilst in 1934 they were employed to level and widen the paths on both the Whitcliffe and the Castle Walks.[14]

In 1933, following a public meeting to discuss the plight of the unemployed, a call went out to other citizens in the town to try and find work for them. Shopkeepers and other employers were asked to look at their staffing levels to see if they could take on an extra worker. In a special supplement issued in the local newspaper entitled 'Spend For

HARVEST – CASTLE
Ludlow served a farming community that came right up to, and sometimes inside, the borough boundary. As well as offering full-time work to many men, the farming year also offered part-time work to all members of the family that allowed them to earn extra income. This could be sowing in the springtime, helping out at the harvest or picking potatoes. Farmers were transporting such workers to their farms daily in 1960. (Courtesy of Shropshire Museum Service)

Prosperity,' better-off householders in the borough were asked to peruse a list of possible work that they could have carried out. Suggestions included having their golf kit renovated, new loose covers made for their furnishings, having a new carpet for their car fitted or having their clocks cleaned or repaired: a list that highlighted the economic gulf in the town.[15]

The depth of poverty that a few families had to endure was considerable. For example, when a five-week-old girl died at 9 Frog Lane in 1886, the father, Cornelius Everall, asked for the baby to be buried at the Union expense as he could not

COAL DRAY
Coal was the main fuel for heating and cooking but since few cottages had storage space coal had to be ordered every two or three weeks. Because the coal cupboard was often in the scullery or under the stairs, deliveries often had to be carried through the house. The sight of the horse drawn coal dray was a common one up to and just after the Second World War. Here a Mr Stokes (possibly George Stokes of Noakes' Yard off Old Street) is seen delivering his sacks (c1910) almost certainly loaded at a coal yard adjacent to the railway station.

(Courtesy of Shropshire Museum Service)

afford the 6/- burial fee. When this was refused he was forced to ask the magistrates for an order to remove and bury the body on health grounds. Finally the Relieving Officer loaned the money to the parents to be paid off in instalments over the coming weeks.[16] Difficulties for many families in being able to bury their dead without being put into debt carried over into the twentieth century. Burial fees at the new council cemetery on Henley Road were £1, and this applied even to babies who lived for over ten minutes. Parents would also have to pay a further 2/6d for the hire of the bier. Councillor Poyner informed his committee that *'there was a poor man in the town who had just buried two infants within a few days of each other and had to pay twice.'* If the church bell was tolled then a further 5/- would have to be paid and it was claimed that *'sentiment was so deep-seated in many people that they would rather sell the shirts off their backs than have a child buried without the bell.'*

It was discovered that only 7/6d of the burial fee was the council charge, the other 12/6d being levied by the church along with the payment for the gravedigger. In the light of this problem the council said they would at least review their charge and also include the use of the bier in any reduced fee. They could not speak for the church.[17]

Clothing the Poor

When just being able to put food on the table was often difficult, keeping a family in clothes was also very hard. One charity tried to help out in this respect during the nineteenth century: the Ludlow Winter Clothing Society. Financed by subscriptions, it provided clothes for the really needy but mainly acted as a clothing club. It encouraged and accepted small weekly payments from the poor so that they could accumulate enough savings to be able to purchase new clothes when it became necessary.[18]

By the twentieth century a number of shops and church organisations were running clothing clubs to help poor families save and they were still an integral part of the family budget for many in 1960. Brenda Oliver's mother was a member of the club run by Bon Marche of Corve Street as was Jean Parker's mother, whilst Michael Newman's mother was a member of Dan Slack's clothing club.

In the 1950s Elfreda Sampson, with two young daughters to clothe, paid into two clubs: those run by Poyners of Broad Street and Williams of the High Street. Winifred Howard had a slightly different experience. She was given money each week to take to her Sunday school and the amount saved could then be used to purchase items from a number of participating outlets. When the day came to spend the monies it was an experience to be appreciated and remembered. Margaret McGarrity recalled that every Easter she and her sisters got *'a new dress, new white socks and new sandals. We didn't have shoes as such. We always had plimsolls or sandals because they were the cheapest thing you could get.'* Shoes were a treat. When Sheila Smith had some bought for her *'you would look at the box for ages.'* New clothes were also a highlight for Susan Jones and her sisters who, each year, looked forward avidly to receiving a new summer dress.

Most clothes that those interviewed received were second-hand ones and often hand-me-downs from elder siblings as Michael Newman, Susan Jones, Freda Stewart and Winifrid Howard all recall. Neighbours also often helped out when their youngest had no one to hand down their clothes to, whilst Jean Parker, being the eldest, 'had me cousin's hand-me-downs.'

Other clothes were bought at jumble sales and then altered to fit as was done by Brenda Oliver's mother. In the 1930s, Freda Stewart's mother bought many of her nine children's clothes second-hand from a woman the children called 'Apple Annie' who lived on the corner of Holdgate Fee and St John's Road. In the late 1950s and early 1960s Jean Parker's mother, in addition to going to jumble sales, also visited a lady known to all as 'Aunt Tilly,' a dealer in rags and second-hand clothes, who operated from a shed at the top of her garden in Old Street. Her mother would also buy old woollen jumpers from her and then unpick them to knit fresh ones for her children. Being an only child, Jean Taylor received no hand-me-downs. *'I didn't have many clothes. My Mum would wash my dress at night and I would wear it the next day.'* In large families, like the Stewarts of Holdgate Fee, shoes were also handed down with repairs often carried out by the father in order to save money. Hobnails were also put into the soles of boys' boots to make them last longer.

FIRE IN LOWER BROAD STREET
In 1908, a fire broke out at the furniture storage warehouse of Bodenham and Sons at the bottom of Lower Broad Street. Worried that the fire could spread, those families living close by brought their treasured belongings out onto the street. It is interesting to note what they wished to save: favourite armchairs, bedding, an umbrella and a decorated biscuit barrel. This is an indication of what little of material value they had in their homes. (Courtesy of Shropshire Museum Service)

The Weekly Menu

Even in the 1950s the food eaten by most working class families in Ludlow tended to be plain and the occasional change deemed a treat. Sunday lunch, or dinner as it was called then, was the main meal of the week. As Winifrid Howard, who was brought up at the bottom of Old Street, explained, this usually consisted of a cheap cut of meat with vegetables. The uneaten meat then formed the base for the main meal for the next few days.

On the Monday, usually washday, any leftover meat was served cold and then any bones used as the base of a stew that often lasted two days. Now and again they would have fish and chips with the three fish cut up so that the whole family could have some. The staple filling food consumed all week was bread covered with lard, jam or dripping. The dripping could be purchased from the Feathers Hotel for three pence whilst on some occasions a jug of soup could be purchased from the Salvation Army. The evidence of Joe Griffiths, who spent his childhood in Central Hall Yard, Upper Galdeford, is very similar. For his family too the main meal of the week was the midday Sunday meal. Cooked meals were also eaten every evening with the whole family sitting down together at the table; stew being the most common dish served.

Lunch was always self-service with the usual bread and jam or dripping. The experience of Jean Parker throughout the late 1950s and early 1960s was very similar. She also recalls that midweek meals mainly comprised lots of stews often with a rabbit base. They also ate a lot of egg and chips. Fridays, being father's payday, always stood out since that was when they had chips from the shop. *'That was our treat and we also had a bar of chocolate from the pub.'* Rabbit, often having been poached, was, it appears, a very common dish served in working-class homes. As Brenda Oliver simply but eloquently put it: *'we had it roasted, boiled, everyway. It was the Sunday joint.'* They even got 6d for each rabbit skin from a Mrs Adams on the Monday. George Cox boasted that, from the age of nine, he could catch a rabbit. He also makes one other interesting point, that as more and more schoolchildren began having a cooked midday meal at school, once home in the evening they now tended to have a cold tea based on the usual bread, jam or dripping, with sometimes a cake to follow or occasionally a bag of chips from the shop. The same change to a hot lunch or dinner at school and a bread and jam tea was experienced by Susan Jones and her sisters.

One further way that families added to their diet was by rearing and slaughtering pigs and then using every part of the animal to help feed the family. Both Sheila Stephens and Michael Newman recalled that children watched with vicarious pleasure when the slaughterman came to kill a local

THE LELLO CHILDREN
In 1928, when their father was given the job of resident engineer at the electricity generating plant by the side of Dinham Bridge, the Lello children moved from Lower Galdeford to Dinham Cottage. Pictured here, from left to right, are Cyril, Ted, Harold, Les and Winnie. Due to the lack of a bathroom, no running hot water and being unable to afford many new clothes, it is clear how difficult it was to keep children clean. However, this did not stop Cyril going on to play professional football for Everton and England.
(Courtesy of Scenesetters)

SHOP IN BELL LANE
Working class areas had a number of small shops to supply most of their everyday needs. With no pantry and no way of keeping anything fresh, food had to be purchased and used daily. This shop in Bell Lane, at the turn of the twentieth century, is typical with the business on the ground floor of the property and the owner living above.
(Courtesy of Ludlow Historical Research Group)

pig. Some were hung up by their back legs so after its throat was cut the blood could be drained off to make black pudding. Sheila remembered that *'all us kids used to think it was fantastic. The poor thing used to squeal.'* When it was dead its hair was singed off and then the carcass scalded and scraped. Some pigs would be held down on a board by three of four men whilst the throats were cut as Don Burmingham witnessed. These killings were usually carried out on a Saturday. The pig would then be carried indoors to be hung from a hook in the ceiling: the hall in Don Burmingham's grandfather's house in Old Street and the back kitchen at Sheila Burmingham's parents' council house on Sandpits Avenue. Here, the same day, just as it had been done since medieval days, the belly would be split open and the intestines removed for washing. The bladder would be given to local children to use as a football. A 'belly stick' would then be placed in the carcass keeping the sides apart and allowing the air to circulate to enable cooling and setting. Then, on the Monday, the pig was taken down, laid on a marble slab, and the slaughterman would call to cut the pig up. The meat would then be salted and the hams and flitches hung from hooks to be used as and when.

Sheila Burmingham remembers how the family food budget was supplemented by using every part of the animal. The fat was cut into cubes and then melted in order to make lard. After the 'scratchings' were removed the fat was allowed to cool in a large pot and then the resultant lard could be spooned out over the coming weeks and months as and when necessary. The lungs and liver were used to help make faggots with the membrane of the stomach utilised to hold the ingredients together. The intestines or 'chitlins', after initial washing, were soaked in salted water that was changed twice a day for the first week and once a day during the second. Each time a 'chitling stick' was pushed through the intestine and used to turn it inside out. After two weeks the chitlins were ready for eating. As for the head this was boiled and then scraped and this flesh was added to the chopped up tongue to make brawn. The brain was eaten on toast or, in order to make it go further, Sheila's mother added breadcrumbs and fried it with bacon. The feet or 'trotters' provided further meals.

On the Slate

To survive each week many housewives had to ask for credit until payday. Margaret McGarrity was often told to *'go up to Mr Jones the baker and ask him if he will let me have a loaf of bread until Friday when we got the pay, and he would put it in a little book.'* Freda Stewart's mother had a slate at her local grocer that she also settled each payday. Freda also recalls that credit would also be given by 'packmen' who went from door to door hawking various goods. Payment could be made by instalments and be collected at each subsequent visit. Marilyn Weaver, whose mother ran a small grocery shop in Market Street, saw all of this from the other side. She recalls her mother giving a number of customers credit until the end of the week.

Holidays

With money always having to be carefully watched, holidays were something that few working-class people in Ludlow experienced. It was not until the *Bank Holiday Act 1871* that workers received any holidays at all and though by the twentieth century most employees received a holiday of one week a year, it was unpaid. Governments attempted to introduce legislation in 1925, 1929 and 1936 to ensure all workers received at least one week's paid holiday, but all failed. By this time only 1.3 million workers had achieved this goal and that was through trades union pressure but other than on the railways, most of Ludlow's workers were not unionised. Even when the *Holidays with Pay Act 1938* was finally passed in 1939, other than for the workers in industries where a Trades Board set a minimum wage, the Act only recommended employers to pay wages. This meant that in Ludlow, for the overwhelming majority of workers, paid holidays only came into being after the Second World War.[19]

Most of those interviewed, who were mainly born in the 1930s and 1940s, can only remember having occasional days out usually organised by some local group. Michael Newman and Joe Griffiths recall being taken out for the day by their respective Sunday schools, in the case of Michael to the North Wales coast. For George Cox the organised trip

BAKERS

Bread was another commodity that had to be purchased daily. In 1911 Ludlow had nine bake houses supplying the town with bread. These bakers (c1912) worked for Marstons who had premises next door to the Feathers Hotel. Work would start in the early hours of each morning and the freshly baked loaves would then be taken from here to various shops and businesses by horse drawn delivery carts.

(Courtesy of Shropshire Museum Service)

was to Porthcawl. Susan Jones was also taken to the Welsh Coast on trips organised by the Rocks Spring Baptist Church. For Brenda Oliver it was a day out by train to Barry Island or New Brighton, organised for the families of railway employees. As for more than a day away Brenda went to a farm at Craven Arms or to an uncle's just south of Hereford whilst the first extended holiday away from Ludlow enjoyed by Philip Sadler was as a teenager in the late 1950s when he went to Bournemouth.

For many young men, however, the very first time they actually spent a night outside the town was when they were called up for National Service. This was the experience of George Cox, Michael Newman and John Marsh. It was even later for Jean Parker whose first night away from Ludlow was on her honeymoon in 1976: two nights at Rhyl.

Prostitution in Ludlow

For families living week-by-week, earning extra income was not only a necessity where the breadwinner was unemployed but in a low-wage town was a constant need for many. During the nineteenth century in particular, this drove many women into prostitution. Measuring how common prostitution was in the town is not easy but it appears to have been quite extensive. The Blue Book of Judicial Statistics for the county in 1865 lists eight brothels in Ludlow. In addition, the police charge books for the period 1865-1882 still survive though the detail they give varies greatly. More often than not, the occupations of the people charged is not listed nor their full addresses, just the charge and any subsequent action or sentence.

However, occasionally, when a woman is a known prostitute, even if the charge is drunkenness, assault, abusive language or even theft, this has sometimes been noted. In this way 61 women can be identified as prostitutes though this number is certainly a gross underestimation. In addition, four persons were charged with keeping a brothel. Using the census returns it is possible to discover the backgrounds of some of the women although, due to a few of them using aliases (again noted in the charge book) or later marrying or taking the name of a common-law husband, a number have proved difficult to trace.[20] For those found, some light is shed regarding the personal circumstances of these women.

Most of the full-time prostitutes tended to be single young women, especially those that worked in the small, cottage-based brothels that were situated in areas such as Lower and Upper Galdeford, Raven Lane, Silk Mill Lane and St John's Lane.[21] Others were part-time and in this category could be found married women with children who appear to have gone on the streets to bring in extra income at times when money was short, possibly due to their husband's unemployment. A number of women appear to fit into this category such as Mary Ann Langford, aged 42, who lived in Corve Street in 1871 with her husband and four children, and also Jane Penny, aged 34, who in 1881 lived with her labourer husband and six children also in Corve Street. Other wives who were forced to sell sex were those whose husbands had left Ludlow in search of work and had either failed or been unable to send monies to their family. Eliza Booth of Lower Galdeford, was one of these women. Eliza, aged 28, who had to house and feed three children whilst her husband was away, lived with her married sister who appears to have been in the same unfortunate position as her.

Another group where a number sometimes felt compelled to become prostitutes in order to support themselves were widows, especially those with children. Sarah Hotchkiss of Lower Galdeford, widowed in her thirties and left to bring up a son, began soliciting to bring in income whilst

WAIT'S SHOP – LOWER CORVE STREET
This is Wait and Sons, bakers and grocers of Lower Corve Street. Such shops often provided the credit that some families required. With many mouths to feed and with low wages often being earned by a husband, a housewife may run short of money. A number of shopkeepers would allow customers to purchase goods 'on the slate' writing down the amount owed in a notebook. At the end of the week, on payday, the outstanding amount would be settled.
(Courtesy of Shropshire Museum Service)

Milborough Hince, who was also widowed while living in Lower Galdeford and left with four children to support, chose a slightly different route. Milborough became a brothel keeper in the 1860s and 70s and took in three young prostitutes who worked for her.

Prostitution was, in many ways, a service industry for the outlying districts. The customers, according to the police charge books, mostly appear to have been from the surrounding villages: farmers, farm labourers and waggoners. These men, visiting Ludlow, were away from the watchful gaze of their wives and girlfriends or the prying eyes of fellow villagers. And the main occasions for the prostitutes to ply their trade were the many market and fair days. Cattle, sheep and pigs were bought and sold in the Bull Ring until 1860 when the markets were transferred to the Smithfield. These sales were held in February, August, September, December and at Easter and Whitsun. Then there were the horse fairs

PHEASANT INN

Thomas Sheldon, the landlord of the Pheasant Inn, situated on the corner of Tower Street and Old Street, poses with his family (c1910). In 1851 Ludlow had 71 public houses and in 1900 there were still 43, one for just fewer than one hundred of the residents. The reason for so many was that they were the main source of entertainment for working people, especially the men. If the choice, after a hard day's work, was between staying in a crowded, damp and dimly lit cottage or sitting in a warm bar with friends then the latter usually won.

(Courtesy of Ludlow Historical Research Group)

COLLIER'S SHOP ON OLD STREET

Ina Collier's (known as Ma Collier's) shop at 87, Old Street, close to Friar's Walk, catered for the needs of working class families. A few yards uphill had been the two slum areas of Dean's Yard and Noakes' Yard, only finally demolished in 1937, whilst opposite was to be found Frog Lane (St John's Road), the home of many families of hawkers and general dealers. Further down the street were the cottages and yards of Holdgate Fee. It is claimed that when anyone entered the shop the owner's parrot would cry out "Shop."

(Courtesy of Ludlow Historical Research Group)

that returned to Mill Street and Castle Square in 1890 and the annual poultry fair each December. In addition, butter and cheese fairs were held quarterly and there was an annual hop fair. There was also the May fair that had originally been for the hiring of labourers and servants, a weekly Monday market for grain, poultry and general provisions as well as weekly provision markets on Wednesday, Friday and Saturday.[22] Each one brought possible clients to town.

Other extra income

Other families brought in extra income in more respectable ways. Being residents in an agricultural market town, many in Ludlow worked on farms during periods such as harvest, and this included women and children. In both the boys' and the girls' sections of the National School on Lower Galdeford absences due to pupils working on the land to earn extra money for their families was taken for granted. The summer

TWO CLASSES

The Broadgate in some ways divided the classes on the south side of the town with most of the poorer sections outside the old town walls. This c1900 photograph captures this. On the left you have the women who lived in the cottages of Lower Broad Street, many aged before their time due to the hardships of bringing up a family on little money. On the right, in the pony trap, are two middle class ladies in their fine coats on their way through the arch to a life made more comfortable by the employment of servants. (Courtesy of Shropshire Museum Service)

break was known as the harvest vacation and when school officially reopened the school logbook of 1863 showed that it was expected that over 20% of the pupils would still be working and therefore missing from classes. For some it was late October before they returned.[23]

Even when education became compulsory, little changed, as many families often had to put the extra income above the importance of schooling for their children. Throughout the last quarter of the nineteenth century parents were taken to court in batches for failing to send their children to school: 38 families were prosecuted in September/October 1878 alone and 28 in February 1880. It is of no surprise that their addresses were all in the poorer working-class areas of the town.[24]

Life on the Edge of Poverty 141

Such absences still occurred in the 1950s. September was hop-picking time and Rusty Matthews along with his mother and most other families on and near St John's Road were picked up in an old army lorry and taken to the hop fields near Tenbury. As he noted: *'Come to think of it the school must have been empty because we all went.'* It was the same in the interwar years. In addition, if families, such as that of Joseph Griffiths' mother, were employed in hop fields some distance away then they would stay along with other families, many from the Black Country, sleeping and living in long lines of huts. Although the work was hard and conditions often spartan, it was looked forward to as part-holiday, away from the usual daily life. For two weeks every year this was the experience of Freda Stewart's family. Along with her mother,

HOP PICKING

One way that families earned extra income was to go hop picking. September was hop-picking time and from Ludlow most would travel to the hop fields near Tenbury. If daily travel were not possible then families would stay in long lines of huts provided by the farmer communally living alongside many families from the Black Country. For children this meant a further two weeks off school each year. The annual hop-picking exodus was still happening in the 1950s.

(Courtesy of Shropshire Museum Service)

brothers and sisters she went hop picking and stayed in the huts provided, with cooking carried out on a communal outside fire.

Potato and fruit picking on local farms was another way of earning extra cash for the family and had been throughout the years. Susan Jones went fruit picking with her sisters on local farms and would be picked up and taken in a cattle truck. Bob Jones and his siblings also went fruit picking at Ashford Carbonel throughout the 1960s. They were paid in tokens that were exchanged for cash at the end of the season. Meanwhile, his mother picked potatoes. Michael Newman went with his family potato gathering as did Rusty Matthews and Freda Stewart and Joan Thomas. As Joan pointed out: 'We went with Mum. That was our holiday in the summer.'

Joseph Griffiths recalls what this part-time working on the land entailed. The youngest of eight children, Joseph would accompany them and his mother to hoe and thin out various crops in the spring and then pick potatoes, sugar beet or whatever else the farmer had ready in the autumn. If they were at a farm near Steventon they would all walk there, but if the fields were further away then a farmer would hire a bus and pick up workers from most of the houses in Sandpits Avenue. From the nearest road they were then transferred to the chosen field by tractor and trailer. Being the youngest, his first job was to keep the fire lit at the edge of the field so that the women could bake potatoes in it for dinner. On wet days his mother and other women would wear two sacks to try and keep dry and keep mud off their clothes: one sack covered their head and back from the rain whilst they wrapped the other around their lower body and tied it at the waist. Different farmers paid in different ways: some by weight, some by the day and some by the length of the furrow. And the day could be long as they were often picked up at 7am and sometimes worked until it grew dark. A number of men such as Freda

MARKET HALL AND TRADERS
Ludlow was a market town and visitors from the countryside, as well as local people, set up stall almost daily in and around the Market Hall (c1880). If they could not get a place in the hall then they displayed their wares, such as baskets, second hand clothes and fruit and vegetables, outside on the ground. The crowd in the background outside what was then the rectory, many with their umbrellas unfurled on a sunny day, is indicative of the fact that a sunburnt skin was a sign of the working lower classes.
(Courtesy of Shropshire Museum service)

Stewart's father would also go haymaking on local farms after their usual day's work or at weekends. For those who lived near the poverty line, all such extra earnings were a godsend.

Picking wild fruit and other hedgerow plants for sale was also a way of supplementing the family income. The *Ludlow Advertiser* described how whole families went out together into the nearby countryside during the interwar years to pick blackberries, elderberries and winberries that were then sold to the wholesaler Peachey's of Corve Street.[25] They in turn sent them to market in Birmingham or Wolverhampton,

SNOW IN THE BULLRING
With many men in occupations where outside work was the norm, bad weather could result in them being laid off, often for weeks. As a result, unemployment during the winter months soared. Charitable help through soup kitchens and the handing out of tickets to obtain coal and groceries was one way that families were helped. Another was that the local council would offer short-term, paid employment to men on jobs such as clearing snow.
(Courtesy of Shropshire Museum Service)

or jam factories or dye works. This daily exodus, mainly economic, but partly social, carried on in the 1950s as many of those interviewed fondly recalled. The local newspaper also reported about families collecting various herbs and flowers such as foxgloves and star moss from the hedgerows to sell to T B Flemons, of 23 Corve Street, who had a drying kiln behind his premises.[26] Again, this still carried on after the Second World War.

Yet another way in which families supplemented their income was to pluck birds. At the coroner's inquest on a suicide held at the skating rink in Lower Broad Street, the jury heard that before he shot himself, the man, who had been suffering from severe headaches ever since returning from the army

Life on the Edge of Poverty 145

in 1918, had been in the washhouse with his wife dressing fowls.[27] Michael Newman recalls doing the same alongside his mother, father and elder brother at Peachey's, wholesalers, after the Second World War. They could work both in the evenings and at weekends, and at Christmas could be there until midnight. They were paid according to a sliding scale depending on whether the bird was a chicken, duck, turkey or goose.

One further way of generating extra income was the taking-in of Birmingham children who had lost their fathers during the First World War and whose mothers were working

WORKERS – WEALES BUILDERS
These workers belonged to the building firm of Benjamin Weale that built most of the houses in the East Hamlet area in the last quarter of the nineteenth century. What has to be remembered is that these same men would often find themselves laid off when winter came and building work slowed down or even halted. They would then find themselves and their families relying on charity, queuing at the Town Hall soup kitchen and collecting tickets that could be exchanged for coal or groceries.

(Courtesy of Shropshire Museum Service)

CHIPP'S FURNITURE SHOP

Chipp's Furniture Showrooms was to be found on Corve Street (now Swifts the Bakers). Here, in c.1960, two ladies window shop and are probably giving thought to how lucky newly-weds were then compared to themselves when they married in being able to afford such luxuries for their home, even if it was on hire purchase or the 'never-never.'

(Courtesy of Ludlow Historical Research Group)

to keep them fed and clothed. During the school summer holiday period, the children were lodged with local families who were paid for taking them. This was still happening in 1931 when, because of the damage that some of the children caused to the equipment at the Sandpits playing field, council tenants were banned from having them as boarders though it appears that other families still did so.[28]

Throughout the years, because of a low wage economy, many families in Ludlow found it a daily struggle to provide a roof over their heads, food on the table, and clothes on their backs. Local charity helped at times, but extra sources of income often had to be found and prudent housekeeping adhered to. Life could be difficult and especially so for the wife and mother who had to eke out carefully the weekly wage to keep her family together. Until the welfare state was properly established after the Second World War life was also very precarious for those too old to work or those who were unemployed. Daily life for many in Ludlow was hard.

OLD STREET SCHOOL 1929

This class photograph is of pupils attending the British School (built by nonconformists) in Old Street in January 1929. This was an elementary school that gave children a basic education from the age of five until fourteen when they would leave to find work. Many of these children often went both hungry and cold, especially in the winter months, when many of their fathers were laid off from work. In the month this photograph was taken a soup kitchen had to be opened in the Market Hall and school records show many pupil absences caused by them having to queue with their parents both for their bowls of soup and for vouchers to enable them to receive free coal so that families could both heat their homes and cook.

(Courtesy of Linda Rowberry)

CHAPTER SEVEN

The Arrival of the Council House

A few local authorities, governing some of the larger towns and cities, had taken advantage of government legislation in the late nineteenth and twentieth century to demolish slum property and build new homes for the working classes. The majority, however, had not and Ludlow was one of the many. The change was to come in the form of the *Addison Housing Act 1919* which compelled all local authorities to build what became known as council estates to combat housing shortages.[1] Some authorities happily swam with the tide of change whilst others, like Ludlow, at first just tentatively dipped their toe into what they viewed as possibly dangerous, financial waters.

A general election was called immediately after the armistice was signed in November 1918 ending the hostilities of the First Word War. Later that same month, on the electioneering trail, David Lloyd George, speaking in Wolverhampton, proclaimed, 'What is our task? To make Britain a fit country for heroes to live in.' From this moment on 'Homes for Heroes' was one plank of a promised utopia. A lot of groundwork had already been carried out. In July 1917 all local authorities had been asked to investigate the quality and quantity of their housing stock and submit plans

The Arrival of the Council House

for supplying housing schemes to cover any shortfall. Ludlow, along with all other local authorities, did as was asked and, considering the state of working class housing in the borough, they submitted the rather unambitious and tentative plan of building just 22 homes at the bottom of Holdgate Fee.

Nothing was promised, however, until the government decided how the building was to be financed and on whose shoulders any annual loss against rental income would be borne. In February 1919 it was agreed that the local authorities would have to raise the capital but that the Treasury would cover any annual loss over the product of one penny on the local rate which in Ludlow would be approximately £100. With this

COUNCIL HOUSE OPENING

In 1929 a decision was taken to build forty new council houses on a field at the corner of Sandpits Lane and Rock Lane. The mayor, John Palmer, is here opening the first block of four. Though a distinct improvement on many of the dilapidated houses throughout the town they had no indoor lavatory, no hot water system, no washbasin in the bathroom and still had gas lighting. Such amenities had to wait until an improvement programme was slowly embarked upon from 1965.

(Courtesy of Shropshire Museum Service)

LOWER MILL STREET
Though found to be unfit for habitation these six cottages on Lower Mill Street were deemed of historical and architectural significance. To the dismay of the Society for the Protection of Historic Buildings, the council, when the Grammar School wanted to expand, ignored plans to improve and save them whilst still allowing the school to build on the land behind them. In 1959 councillors voted in favour of demolition leaving an open gash that still remains today.

(Courtesy of Ludlow Historical Research Group)

agreed financial guarantee, limiting any possible financial loss that a local authority could suffer, the *Housing Act* was passed. It compelled all councils to build housing estates to alleviate their local housing shortage. Ludlow Council now had no option but to start building.

Still worried over the rising cost of building materials, Ludlow council just put out twelve of the planned houses to tender and then decided to build only eight at first. Their main fear was that many prospective tenants would not be able to afford the rents. It was initially thought that the houses could be let at 4/6d a week but rising post-war costs meant that the weekly rent now proposed was 9/-. This was not the only problem. An outcry had erupted over the site of the new houses. Efforts were being made to have the scheme halted and switched to a higher part of the town such as Rocks Green Road or Sandpits Lane. The Ludlow and District Trades and Labour Council wrote to the Ministry of Health setting out their opposition on health grounds. They argued that the site was in the lowest part of the town and situated next to the gas works that produced a noxious stench at times, and where work went on all night preventing tenants from having a proper rest. In addition, it was close to the river and was prone to flooding and fogs. In fact, they claimed that the houses were being built in the area of the town that had the highest child mortality. Even the local architect for the scheme remarked:

'The site... was chosen before I was called in and it is greatly to be regretted with so many sites in healthy positions and with natural beauty available everywhere that this site was ever sanctioned.'[2] Nevertheless, though it took over three years, the rather meagre number of 22 houses was finally built on Teme Avenue, Holdgate Fee and Temeside.

The fear of many councillors that the higher rents would deter prospective tenants proved unfounded since the number who applied far exceeded the number of houses.[3] However, after the ending of the *1919 Addison Housing Act* and the passing of the *1923 Chamberlain Housing Act*, the council still decided not to build any more but to encourage private builders to use the Act to build. Sadly they did not. This meant that when the first Labour Government of 1924 passed

NEW STREET – 1920s

Photographed in the 1920s standing in New Street, these two young girls were living on the very edge of urban Ludlow as evidenced by the surrounding farmland. After the Second World War this would be where council houses would be constructed that would make up the Dodmore estate.

(Courtesy of Phillip Sadler)

what became known as the *Wheatley Housing Act*, providing an annual subsidy on each house for the next forty years, local pressure to build more council homes increased. In 1925 the council purchased 3½ acres of land on the corner of Henley Road and Sandpits Lane. On this they built 31 new homes, 26 facing Henley Road and six facing Sandpits Lane. The main area of disagreement this time was the size of the houses. It was finally agreed that all would be three bedroomed but only twelve with a parlour. As Alderman Sheldon explained just before the foundation stone was laid in July 1926:

'If I had my way I should certainly have had all the houses of the smaller type, for we are, I take it, building them for the poorer classes.'[4]

The next scheme of 40 new council homes to be built under the same act was to be on a field at the corner of Sandpits Lane and Rock Lane. Planned in early 1929 and to be completed by the end of the year, the new estate was still controversial. Notwithstanding that tenants for all the other houses built had been found, fears still remained that this new scheme could be a white elephant. Alderman Ernest Bodenham, a draper of Broad Street, was still arguing that those that needed rehousing would not be able to afford the rent. He argued that at present they were paying 3/- to 4/- a week whilst the new homes would be 5/6d to 6/-. He doubted, therefore, whether they would be even able to find 40 tenants. Councillor Archibald Cartwright saw where the houses were being built as a disincentive, claiming:

'It would be very difficult to persuade people to leave the houses that they were now living in. They could not drive them into other buildings specially if those buildings were situated far away from the working part of the town.'

Both men were wrong. Eighty applications were received before the building of a single house was even started. Even when all tenants were chosen, nearly 60 families remained disappointed on a waiting list.[5] An editorial in the *Ludlow Advertiser* noted this and pressed the council to accelerate council house building.

'Some of the hovels in Ludlow are a perfect disgrace and the sooner they are condemned and demolished the better. They are a danger to the health of the occupants and a breeding ground for fevers. It is to be hoped that the council will lose no time in tackling this problem that requires their urgent attention. A visit by the Housing Committee to some slums now occupied would convince them of the need for another housing scheme.'[6]

A new housing scheme did result though it was far from radical. A decision was made to build a further 22 houses under the 1924 Housing Act on land that would become

LAYING ELECTRICITY CABLE
Both street and residential lighting in Ludlow was powered by gas until 1906 when a generating station was built on Portcullis Lane that initially fed mains throughout the centre of the town. Slowly the network was expanded and here can be seen a Bristol firm laying cables on Gravel Hill in 1908. For many living in rented cottages, gas, and even oil lamps and candles, still remained the norm for many who only experienced electric lighting when they moved to a council house after the Second World War. Many of the families left residing in the old cottages littered throughout the town still lacked electricity in 1960. (Courtesy of Shropshire Museum Service)

Steventon Crescent. A few voices were still raised against even this small number. Councillor William Parsonage thought their building would be unfair to local landlords who could lose their tenants and their income.[7]

In 1930 a new Housing Act was passed that was designed specifically to rehouse slum dwellers but the council decided not to take advantage of it, a decision that, as seen in Chapter 4, caused the Rector of St Laurence's, the Reverend Channer, to preach his critical sermon on the housing situation and prompted the *Ludlow Advertiser* to undertake a special investigation into the extent of slum housing in the town. Faced with this outcry and a letter from the Ministry, who had been alerted to the situation by the editor of the local newspaper, the council soon rescinded their decision but still managed to drag their feet with the result that no new council homes were built. When pressed in 1933 for a housing plan for the next five years, the councillors replied that as they had built 139 new homes since 1919, they had no plans to build any

ST JOHN'S LANE – TOP

This is St John's Lane where it joins with St John's Road. Though earmarked for demolition for many years, action to remove these cottages, many of which had been deemed unfit for human habitation for decades, only began in the 1970s. In the nineteenth century the lane housed at least one of the brothels that could be found in the poorer areas of the town. Note how narrow the lane is. This was not out of the ordinary before the redevelopment of parts of Ludlow in the second half of the twentieth century. The only building still standing today is the cottage on the right.

(Courtesy of Shropshire Museum Service)

more in the near future. This was in spite of the continuing evidence that more were needed. Harry Didlick of St John's Lane, who had a wife and three children, complained to the magistrate, who was deciding on an eviction order, that the landlord had failed to carry out repairs both to the roof and the drains. The magistrate then asked him why, in that case, had he not moved to a council house. Didlick replied that 'I have been trying for years.' A letter to the *Ludlow Advertiser* supported him. The writer, like many newly-married couples, lived with his in-laws.

'I have been in search of a working class house for over a year without success and there are others in the same position. There is certainly a very great need for more.'[8]

However, it was some years before growing pressure caused the council to provide more houses. The key pressure appears to have come from above: the Ministry of Health. Local pressure could be ignored but Ministry power could only be avoided for a while. After reading the annual reports of Ludlow's MOH, in which the poor quality of the town's housing was being constantly highlighted, it kept asking when action was to be taken. In April 1937 Councillor Mrs Violet Packer strenuously pointed out to the full council that it was better that they took the decision to build rather than have the Ministry order them to do so.

Finally, in January 1938, the council bowed to the inevitable and announced a new scheme of 36 houses to be built along Sandpits Avenue. The clinching argument was that if they did not vote for this scheme then the Ministry could force a more extensive one on them. Better 36 than the feared financial nightmare of far more. The new houses were completed in late 1939 and the beginning of 1940. It also appears that the local housing committee at last realised that Ludlow actually had a housing problem.

This was probably prompted by the house-to-house survey carried out prior to the arrival of hundreds of evacuees on the outbreak of war, carried out by middle-class volunteers, including some councillors and their wives. These people now saw the housing conditions of many of Ludlow's working classes with their own eyes. The council now even went as far as to ask the Ministry to send down an expert to give advice on how they could proceed to alleviate the housing situation.[9] Sadly, the onset of war curtailed any thought of further building in the short term.

WWII and Housing

As the war progressed, the government began to plan for the peace. They ordered all local authorities to prepare an overall plan for the demolition of unfit housing and the building of new properties to rehouse all those displaced and to fill the gap in any existing housing shortage.[10] Ludlow set up a Town Planning and Development Committee to compile a list of condemned properties and to submit possible sites for new council houses.

They came up with six new sites. One, the Smithfield, where it was proposed to build bungalows for older people, was turned down due to the foundations being mounds of rubbish accumulated when it was used as a refuse dump. A second, on land sided by Old Street, St John's Road and St John's Lane was postponed indefinitely as it would have necessitated the demolition of cottages, even though they had already been condemned as unfit for human habitation, in the midst an acute housing shortage. However, the other four sites were built upon in the post-war years though Ludlow still lagged behind other Shropshire towns in the numbers game. By May 1946 Ludlow had only agreed the building of 56 homes compared with 100 at Oswestry, 247 at Bridgnorth and 250 at Shrewsbury. The 56

The Arrival of the Council House

at Ludlow were on three fields comprising 6¼ acres adjoining Dodmore Lane. This delay led to growing impatience in the town as Alderman Violet Packer discovered.

'*Some of the homeless came pleading for houses, some rude and some scurrilous, and she was not surprised that they should be so, for some of them had had their names down for houses since 1939. She knew of places where there were two or three generations living all together in a few rooms and some were sick people.*'[11]

However, homes were soon planned on the other three chosen sites: 12.4 acres of fields at the rear of Sandpits Playing Fields, ½ acre at Temeside left over from the Steventon Crescent scheme, and one acre at Steventon New Road. The initial houses at the Dodmore Lane site were mostly completed by December 1948.

In 1952 a further field abutting the new estate was purchased and built on. At the Sandpits site nine acres of the earmarked land had 80 houses built on it including 56 Airey Houses constructed of prefabricated concrete panels.

HOLDGATE FEE – VIEW DOWNHILL

The state of much of this housing at the southern end of Old Street (once known as Holdgate Fee) was the subject of much concern by various borough surveyors and medical officers of health over the years. Since the end of the Second World War they were part of a proposed slum clearance scheme but they remained standing until the mid 1970s. The large house on Waterside that can be seen in the distance, was the biggest of the many common lodging houses in the town that provided overnight beds for itinerant workers. It was also the last to close, still being open in 1937.

(Courtesy of Shropshire Museum Service)

PIGSTY

The rearing of pigs in the courts, yards and gardens of Ludlow, in order to help feed the family, was a common occurrence and the habit was not broken when families moved into the first council houses. As soon as James Charmer, together with his wife Mary and their six children became the tenants of 21, Steventon Crescent in 1930, he immediately constructed a pigsty near his back door that soon led to the usual, odorous manure heap.

(Courtesy of Jean Parker)

As a result, Riddings Road, Clee View, Wheeler Road and Whitbread Road came into existence. During 1948-52, further schemes on the Sandpits site were planned and carried out providing 58 more houses, and twelve ground floor flats with two-bedroomed maisonettes above them. Seventeen aluminium 'Hawksley' bungalows were also erected on the Steventon Road site.

This sudden spate of council-house building, though it alleviated the housing shortage in the borough, did not solve it. The demand for council homes can be seen in that in March 1949 the housing list had to be temporarily closed because it totalled nearly five hundred and applications were still pouring in. By 1954, and with the completion of many new homes, the waiting list still numbered over three hundred. After decades of under-investment in municipal housing the demand for rented homes was so great that it meant that cottages deemed unfit for habitation many years before still had to be left with tenants inhabiting them.

Improving the Present Housing Stock

Ludlow councillors were offered a second way to alleviate the town's housing problem: renovating and modernising some of the homes deemed unfit for human habitation. This possible solution was initiated by the Ludlow Society (later renamed the Ludlow Civic Society) which was formed in October 1954. They were worried that a number of properties of architectural and historic interest would be lost to the town if the proposed slum clearance schemes went ahead in their entirety. At their invitation a representative of the Society for the Protection of Ancient Buildings visited Ludlow. This organisation was already advising a number of councils and offered Ludlow Council advice on how to apply for grants from the Ministry of Works towards saving chosen buildings.[12] The Town Clerk was now instructed to send the Society a list of the properties within the proposed clearance schemes highlighting those that were either listed under the *Town and Country Planning Act 1947* as of special architectural or historical interest and of those on their supplementary list. These amounted to thirty in the former category and 115 properties in the latter out of a total of 275 properties. The Town Clerk also admitted that this was not a full list.[13]

Once further details requested by the Society had been sent, a Mr Kenneth Reid visited Ludlow in January 1959 to inspect the buildings before preparing a report covering each property. This was sent to Ludlow Council in April 1960. Examples of his suggestions give an indication of his overall strategy to save historic buildings from complete demolition in a way that would help to alleviate the housing shortage whilst keeping or enhancing the townscape. In Lower Broad Street numbers 40-43 would, with discreet partial demolition, be converted into one property whilst numbers 46-50 would become three properties. In Mill Street numbers 11 and 12

PIG
Here, sitting outside the back door of her council house c.1935, Mary Charmer holds a small piglet, purchased to fatten and then to be slaughtered as soon as it was grown. Its killing often became a social event and any neighbours who helped feed it would be there to receive a cut of the meat. The watching children would be thrown the pig's bladder to use as a football. (Courtesy of Jean Parker)

would become one property and numbers 24-26 would become two. In the same way, demolition allied to modernisation would allow numbers 1-9 Lower Mill Street to become three desirable properties. The same careful rebuilding would turn 83-88 Corve Street into two habitable properties.[14]

Sadly, even whilst these plans were being formulated, Ludlow Council was already making decisions to nullify many of them. In March 1959 it was decided to issue demolition orders on the nine properties in Lower Mill Street in order to make room for the expansion of the Boys Grammar School. On being informed the Society in London wrote back to the council that:

'The Society feels that while clearly in need of drastic reconditioning at the present time, they are capable of repair and should be repaired as they are part of an attractive group in this most attractive town.'

They went further and claimed that Reid's plan for the properties could still allow room for the expansion of the Grammar School by demolishing numbers 4,5 and 6 whilst keeping the six listed cottages that fronted the street.[15] Their plea fell on deaf ears and all were demolished. Ironically, where the six cottages stood it is still an open space to this day.

The only real success that emanated from the efforts of the Society was that of the restoration of 46-50 Corve Street. These five cottages, in imminent danger of demolition, were converted successfully into four properties with all amenities and the Mayor was proudly present at their official opening in December 1966. This glimmer of hope, that some of Reid's plans for the renovation of the listed properties would be included as part of the slum clearance schemes, was, sadly, quickly extinguished.

The news that numbers 83-88 Corve Street had been demolished in December 1968 was received with shock in London since Ludlow Council had approved the plans for their renovation ten years before. Kenneth Reid angrily wrote:

'This piece of destruction takes away a couple of 15th-16th century frames apart from later work and also a piece of half timbers that gave a requisite emphasis in this particular streetscape. Besides, its removal will leave a gash and expose the gable end elevation of the public house adjoining, a somewhat gaunt chunk of inelegance. Such won't improve the view of this quarter, especially after the worthy rehabilitation of numbers 46-50 and it also reduces the chance of getting this collection of old Ludlow as a conservation area.'[16]

It was finally clear that after years of delay and prevarication the building of housing estates, not the repair of old Ludlow, was to be the chosen route of Ludlow council for the foreseeable future.

New Council Tenants

As council houses now became a growing part of the townscape it is interesting to note who the new tenants were.[17] It would be thought that they would be those in the greatest need for decent housing but this was not initially the case. Throughout most of the interwar years, although a set of rules was instituted to allow the borough surveyor to list prospective tenants in an order of priority, it appears that the final criterion that councillors used to make their decisive choice was a family's ability to pay the rent, or in their own words 'provided that their financial position is satisfactory.' Some councillors were also worried that if tenants came from slum properties then there was a risk that the new homes 'might soon become a slum.' The result of their choices often led to criticism, even at times from a fellow councillor. When, in 1929, the tenancies of three properties were given to clerks working for the Inland Revenue, George Rogers complained that this 'was not fair to householders who were at present living in places not fit for pigs to live in.' The *Ludlow Advertiser* also called for tenants to be chosen from those living in condemned cottages and then no time should be lost in demolishing 'the numerous hovels … that are not fit for cattle to live in.' Many of Ludlow's citizens could also not understand the final choice of tenants as one letter shows.

'Some of the people provided with houses by the council could very well look after themselves and make room for people in Galdeford, who are still living in conditions that are far from desirable. When the housing scheme was first started I was under the impression that it was mainly intended to provide for people of the working class and with a view to the removal of those who live in dwellings that should long ago have been condemned.'[18]

Though the choice of tenants can be criticized, the aim of the councillors to ensure that bad debts accumulated

The Arrival of the Council House 163

through the failure to collect rents would not fall upon the ratepayers was successful. Taken in conjunction with the almost immediate threat of eviction as soon as any tenant fell behind with payments, the accounts for the year ending March 1937 tell a tale: annual rents collected £2,941-10-6, total rent arrears £2-5-8. Within twelve months even this small figure of rental debt had been totally eradicated.

Evidence that other worries they had regarding tenants had not been entirely inaccurate surfaced after those accepted for the Sandpits Avenue properties in 1939/40 moved in. These were the first where the Government insisted that tenants had to be those rehoused from homes that were deemed as slums. They were chosen from a list made by the borough surveyor of families living in overcrowded conditions or living in unfit houses. Previous habits, however, were difficult to shake off.

ST JOHN'S LANE – BOTTOM

These working class cottages could be found where St John's Lane met Waterside. They were finally demolished in the 1970s as part of a slum clearance scheme that led to the municipal housing development that encompassed the land between St John's Lane to the west, Old Street to the east, St John's Road to the north and Waterside to the south. (Courtesy of Shropshire Museum Service)

Even now the council were warned that they were skating on thin ice as to some of their final choices.

The Borough Surveyor warned them that if they still continued to pick tenants who were not on his list, or ignored specific ones that were, then they ran the risk that the Ministry may take away any agreed subsidy. One example highlighted was a mother with children in Corve Street who, though at the top of his list, was passed over due to concerns over the dirty state of her present property. Even so, very shortly after new tenants moved in, four properties were infested with 'bugs and lice' and required 'fumigating and disinfecting.' Within weeks of the occupation of the new homes the Housing Committee were also asking the police to investigate reports of fighting between tenants. As regards rents, 22 tenants were in arrears within four years even though a number were not being charged the full rents thanks to a government rent rebate scheme.

Amenities in the New Council Houses

The desire to move to a council house was understandable when they were compared to the homes that so many families in Ludlow were forced to live in. Even the very first to be built after the Great War appeared palaces when compared with the cottages hidden away in the courts and yards off Ludlow's streets but they were not yet homes with all the amenities that the middle classes enjoyed.[19]

It was the *Housing Act 1924* that made it compulsory for all council houses to have an indoor bathroom and not just a bath in the scullery. As a result, the first homes built at Teme Avenue and Temeside had to wait until the early 1960s before a modernisation programme not only gave them a bathroom but also hot water and an indoor lavatory. In fact, in 1960, about one hundred of the early interwar council homes

REAR OF HOLDGATE FEE

In 1927, the family of William Harris, a coal merchant whose yard was adjacent to the railway station, poses with his family in the open gardens behind their house on the west side of Holdgate Fee. They were soon to move to a council house in Henley Road being typical of the respectable working class family that could be relied on to pay their rent. Such 'safe' tenants were ones that the housing committee desired in the hope that a filtering up process would then aid other families in search of a better home. Note also the small cottage on the right built on the back of one facing the road thus cutting off much of its light. This was typical of some of the back building carried out to maximise a landlord's income from his plot of land. In addition, pigeon breeding and racing was a popular pastime among Ludlow's working classes at this time and the two boys are obviously being introduced to the joys of the hobby. (Courtesy of Shropshire Museum Service)

were not supplied with a hot water system, having only a gas copper boiler in their bathroom as their sole source of hot water. These included eleven homes in Henley Road, six in Sandpits Road, 22 in Steventon Crescent and 64 in Sandpits Avenue. A pilot scheme to install such a system was begun in 1965 and, in addition, they were to have a small washbasin in each bathroom for the first time. Outside lavatories were also the norm for the early council houses and when they started to become integral to the house, they had to be entered from outdoors. Part of the reason for the modernization programme was embarrassment. As the Housing Committee stated:

'It is imperative for the Council to proceed with the scheme as pressure could hardly be put on private owners to improve their properties if the Council was not itself improving its dwellings.'

Despite this plea, it was still some years before all homes were modernised. Susan Jones, who moved to Sandpits

Avenue in 1961, still had just a cold-water tap in the back kitchen until the early 1970s when, at last, a hot water system was installed.

Lighting in the early council homes was still gas. When Joan Thomas and her parents moved in 1937 to one of the early council houses that had just become vacant on Sandpits Avenue, it was still just lit by gas, though this was an improvement on their one-up, one-down cottage in Lower Galdeford where they still relied on oil lamps and candles. The excitement and joy of the move is still recalled nearly eighty years later.

'Everybody came to see it because we had two bedrooms and we had a kitchen and a big garden and we had our own toilet. Everybody from Galdeford came to see it: the family and the neighbours.'

Until the Sandpits Avenue and Steventon Crescent schemes were planned in 1937/38, the local Gas Company had a monopoly in providing both fuel and lighting to all council homes. This monopoly was finally broken when the Electricity Company offered to pay for all the installation works, not charging the council a penny, and recouping its money over the long term through a meter in each home.

For the new tenants, coming from properties that were often lit by a single gas mantle in the main room and with oil lamps or candles sufficing elsewhere such as in the bedrooms, the effect appeared magical, especially for the children. For Freda Stewart, moving from a cottage in Old Street to Sandpits Avenue in 1939/40, her joy was unbounded as she recalls that *'we couldn't get over switching the lights on and off.'*

It was the same for Margaret McGarrity when she moved with her parents and siblings from Taylor's Court, tucked away off Lower Broad Street, to a new home on the Dodmore Estate in 1952.

'We went in. I can feel it now. We run in. "Mum," I said.

46-50 LOWER CORVE STREET
These five condemned cottages at 46-50 Lower Corve Steet were some of the very few that the council, on the advice of the Society for the Protection of Historic Buildings, decided to restore and modernise rather than demolish. They were converted into four properties with all modern conveniences and officially opened in 1965. They still remain as part of the social housing stock whilst enriching the streetscape.
(Courtesy of Shropshire Museum Service)

"There's a new cooker. Look at this, the lights are coming on." We pulled the switch up and down.'

The whole experience of a new home with so many amenities that they had never had before was a moment to treasure for many of the new tenants. *'It was absolutely wonderful ... Oh it was lovely'* was the memory of Winifrid Howard, when she realised that not only did the house have electric lights but also water taps indoors and not just a single tap but also a hot and a cold one.

The family, for the first time, also had a walk-in pantry with a marble slab to keep food cool and a meat safe with a mesh-covered door to keep the flies away. Brenda Oliver, moving from Lower Corve Street to the Dodmore Estate in 1948 also recalls the joyful shock at such a sudden change from living in an old, overcrowded home.

'It was like Buckingham Palace. You got running water and you could pull the chain in the house. It was luxury. It was absolute heaven. Us two girls had a room of our own.'

And it was not just children who experienced the difference in the quality of living. It is easy to underestimate the change that now occurred in the daily life of a family that a move to a new council property brought. Moving to a council house for many was a move up the social ladder. As a result Brenda's mother left her brass bedstead behind.

'When we were allocated up here, my mother wouldn't bring it because it wasn't good enough. Oh, we can't take that.'

Freda Stewart also recalls her mother's joy at the change in her everyday life that her new home would bring.

ST MARY'S LANE TURNING OFF CORVE STREET

The cottages in the centre, Nos. 83-88 Corve Street, were situated at the junction with St Mary's Lane. Brenda Oliver (nee Massam) spent her childhood at No. 85 until her family moved to a council house in 1948. Not only did none of these properties have electricity but also they had no gas. Lighting was by oil lamps or candles. All cooking still had to be carried out on the coal fired, black leaded cooking range in the main room. The cottages were finally demolished in 1968, rather than being modernised, much to the frustration of the Society for the Protection of Historic Buildings as they dated back to the 15th and 16th centuries.

(Courtesy of Shropshire Museum Service)

'Everything was inside. It was lovely. Mum thought it was great because she didn't have to keep going down the yard.'

Although in the immediate postwar years council houses were being built in greater numbers, the housing shortage in Ludlow meant that any slum-clearance schemes had to be put on hold as any displaced families would have nowhere to move to.[20] In October 1954 the council made this official when all slum-clearance programmes were deferred until further notice. Within two months this decision had to be rescinded when the *Housing Repairs and Rents Act* asked for all local authorities to submit details of their slum-clearance programme. As was seen in Chapter 4, the council now studied a list of properties that the Borough Surveyor and the MOH deemed should be demolished and they agreed that a total of 236 houses should be part of a slum-clearance scheme. However, still no action was taken and decisions were continually put off.

By 1957 matters were even worse. The Borough Surveyor warned the Housing Committee that houses not originally included in the list of properties that required demolition had deteriorated so much that they should now be included. By 1960 the situation had not altered.

The housing scheme planned for Jack's Meadow situated with Old Street to the east, St John's Lane to the west, St John's Road to the north and Temeside to the south envisaged back in 1944 was still on the drawing board and would remain there for at least ten more years. This meant that properties that edged this proposed development, many of which had been condemned as unfit for human habitation before the First World War, were still inhabited. The lack of building also meant that 430 families remained on the council house waiting list and the Ministry of Housing claimed that 250 of these were at present living in properties unfit for human habitation.

The decade of the Beatles, Carnaby Street, the mini-skirt and Flower Power was dawning, but for far too many families in Ludlow, living conditions had altered little since the end of the previous century. Many still had no electricity, many still shared outside water taps whilst running hot water was, for them, still a dream. Numerous families had the often cold and damp walk to outside, shared lavatories which meant that the use of chamber pots at night was still the norm. Admittedly, council houses were now being built but not in enough numbers.

As a result, Ludlow still suffered a housing shortage that meant so many still had to live in dilapidated, rented properties which had been condemned unfit for human habitation long ago.

The beauty of Ludlow's fine houses, which drew tourists to the town, still hid many pockets of poverty and poor living conditions.

Footnotes

CHAPTER ONE

1   For many of the dates of construction see David J Lloyd, 'Property, ownership and improvement in Ludlow, a fashionable country town, 1660-1848' PhD thesis (University of Wolverhampton, 2005).
2   *Nottingham Evening Post* 11 January 1879 and Ludlow Borough Police Charge Book 1872-1882 held at Ludlow Museum and Resource Centre.
3   *Ludlow Advertiser* 19 August and 9 September 1905.
4   *Hereford Times* 18 February 1899
5   Register of Common Lodging Houses under Act of 1851: 1865/66 held at Ludlow Museum and Resource Centre.
6   Reports of the Sanitary Committee to the Town Council 15 February 1886 in Shropshire Archives DA3/106/1.
7   *Ludlow Advertiser* 5 May 1900.
8   *The Story of Ludlow Workhouse* by Derek Williams (Logaston, 2012) and monthly reports of the Board of Guardians in *Ludlow Advertiser.*
9   Registers of Pedlars Certificates in Ludlow Museum and Resource Centre.
10 'Employment and Society in Ludlow' by David Lloyd in *Victorian Ludlow* edited by Ludlow Historical Research Group (Bucknell, 2004).
11 *Ludlow Advertiser* 1 October 1937.

CHAPTER TWO

1   Nuisance Report Books 1861-1871 in Ludlow Museum and Resource Centre.
2   MOH report 1877 in Shropshire Archives PL9/38/2/2 and Report of the Sanitary and General Purposes Committee to the Town Council 1883-1886 in Shropshire Archives DA3/106/1.
3   Report of the Sanitary and General Purposes Committee *op.cit.* and Nuisance Report Books 1861-1871. *op.cit.* 23 November 1865 and 11 August 1871.
4   Nuisance Report Books 1861-1871 *op.cit.* 19 May 1864 and 22 July 1865.
5   Nuisance Report Books 1861-1871 *op.cit.* 9 May 1866; and *Ludlow Advertiser* 5 February 1898 and 8 September 1900.
6   Nuisance Report Books 1861-1871 *op.cit.* 28 June 1868, 11 August 1871 and 26 November 1864 and *Ludlow Advertiser* 8 July 1905.

7   Nuisance Report Books 1861-1871 *op.cit.* 27 December 1865 and 29 July 1866.

8   Nuisance Report Book 1861-1871 *op.cit.* 23 November 1865, 6 May 1864 and 30 September 1863; *Ludlow Advertiser* 3 August 1901 and 9 May 1903.

9   Report of the Sanitary and General Purposes Committee 1883-1886 *op.cit.* and *Ludlow Advertiser* 8 July 1905.

10   *Ludlow Advertiser* 9 May 1903.

11   Evidence given to Ministry of Health Public Enquiry into siting of new Isolation Hospital *Ludlow Advertiser* 11 February 1922.

12   *Ludlow Advertiser* 5 February 1898 and 4 February 1899.

13   *Ludlow Advertiser* 4 February 1920.

14   *Ludlow Advertiser* 9 May 1903 and 16 May 1903.

15   Reports of the Borough Surveyor on Nuisances and Unfit Housing 1908-1911 in Shropshire Archives DA3/802/1-8; *Ludlow Advertiser* 8 February 1908, 9 May 1908, 3 April 1909, 14 January 1913 and 4 December 1920.

CHAPTER THREE

1   *Ludlow Advertiser* 3 January 1863.

2   *Ludlow Advertiser* 7 March 1863, Nuisance Report Book 31 July 1865, Ludlow Museum and Resource Centre and Local Board of Health Minute Book 1859-1878 11 August 1865, 4 June 1868, 5 May 1870 and 7 December 1871, Shropshire Archives DA3/990/1/1.

3   Henry Baker, 'The Coming of Ludlow's Water' in *Shropshire Magazine* 1985 pp. 38-39, Ron Kitchener 'Water Pure Water' *Ludlow Heritage News* No. 20 Autumn/Winter 1993 pp. 2-3 and Martin Speight, 'The Provision of Local Government Services in Ludlow 1830-1880' in *Victorian Ludlow* edited Ludlow Historical Research Society (Bucknell, 2004).

4   Derek Williams, *The Story of Ludlow Workhouse* (Logaston Press, 2012).

5   *Ludlow Advertiser* 25 October 1884.

6   *Ludlow Advertiser* 8 January 1898.

7   *Ludlow Advertiser* 22 July 1948.

8   Housing Committee Minutes 14 June 1955. (In author's possession)

9   *Ludlow Advertiser* 24 October 1922.

10   *Ludlow and Leominster Herald* 19 November 1875.

11   Derrick Banks, 'As You Were' in *Ludlow Heritage News* No 14 Autumn/Winter 1990.

CHAPTER FOUR

1   *Ludlow Advertiser* 5 February 1898.

2   *Ludlow Advertiser* 7 January 1899 and 11 November 1899.

3   *Ludlow Advertiser* 9 December 1899.
4   *Ludlow Advertiser* 6 December 1902.
5   *Ludlow Advertiser* 7 August 1906.
6   *Ludlow Advertiser* 14 June 1913.
7   *Ludlow Advertiser* 12 and 17 November 1921 and 8 April 1922.
8   *Ludlow Advertiser* 12 April 1930.
9   *Ludlow Advertiser* 17 January 1931.
10 *Ludlow Advertiser* 24 January 1931.
11 Entered by a passageway by the side of No 32, Mill Street.
12 *Ludlow Advertiser* 24 January 1931.
13 *Ludlow Advertiser* 14 February 1931.
14 *Ludlow Advertiser* 4 June 1937 and 14 January 1938.
15 *Ludlow Advertiser* 21 June 1946.
16 Ludlow Borough Council Housing Committee Minutes for 1943-45 in author's possession.
17 *Ibid* January to June 1955
18 *Ludlow Advertiser* 4 December 1926 and 15 February 1930.
19 *Ludlow Advertiser* 15 December 1933.
20 *Ludlow Advertiser* 14 October 1922 and 3 October 1937.
21 *Ludlow Advertiser* 14 January and 14 April 1876, 18 November 1922, 13 September 1930 and 18 November 1948.

CHAPTER FIVE

1   'The Provision of Local Government Services in Ludlow 1830-1880' by Martin Speight in *Victorian Ludlow* by Ludlow Historical Research Group (Bucknell, 2004), *Ludlow Advertiser* 25 October 1884 and MOH report for 1899 in *Ludlow Advertiser* 1 March 1900.
2   A.E. Johnson,'Primary and Secondary Education in Ludlow in the 19th Century,' Dissertation1970 in Ludlow Library Local History Collection.
3   *Ludlow Advertiser* 6 February 1902 and 3 May 1902.
4   *Ludlow Advertiser* 7 March 1903.
5   *Ludlow Advertiser* 6 August and 8 October 1904; 8 July 1905; 6 April 1912 and 8 December 1933.
6   *Ludlow Advertiser* 1 March 1900, 4 January 1913 and 4 April 1920.
7   *Ludlow Advertiser* 3 September and 8 October 1921; 4 February 1922 and MOH Report for 1921 in Ludlow Advertiser 8 July 1922.
8   *Ludlow Advertiser* 6 May 1922.
9   MOH Report 1922 and council reaction in *Ludlow Advertiser* 3 March 1923.
10 Martin Pugh, *We Danced All Night: A Social History of Britain Between the Wars* (London, 2008) Chapter 3.

11 MOH Report for 1899 in *Ludlow Advertiser* 1 March 1900.
12 MOH Report for 1912 in *Ludlow Advertiser* 14 June 1913.
13 MOH Report for 1925 in Shropshire Archives ref. DA3/880/4.
14 MOH Report for 1933 in *Ludlow Advertiser* 3 August 1934.
15 *Ludlow Advertiser* 18 January 1935.
16 Culled from MOH Annual Reports reported in *Ludlow Advertiser* and Shropshire Archives DA3/880/1-8.
17 *Ludlow Advertiser* 7 June 1862 and Nuisance Report Book 19 August 1863 in Ludlow Museum and Resource Centre.
18 *Ludlow Advertiser* 6 October 1894 and *Ludlow and Leominster Herald* 3 December 1875.
19 *Ludlow Advertiser* 4 April 1925.
20 Nuisance Report Books 1862-1871 in Ludlow Museum and Resource Centre and *Ludlow Advertiser* 14 June 1913 and 4 April 1925.
21 Ludlow Charitable Reports 1869-72 and 1875-89 in Ludlow Library Local History Collection and *Ludlow Advertiser* 19 March 1932.
22 Pugh, *We Danced All Night op.cit.* Chapter 3.
23 Annual MOH Reports in *Ludlow Advertiser*.
24 *Hereford Times* 18 April 1857; *Ludlow Advertiser* 8 August 1862; *Shrewsbury Chronicle* 31 May 1872; *Ludlow Advertiser* 16 July 1892, *Derby Journal* 7 April 1893 and *London Daily News* 11 November 1904.
25 *Ludlow Advertiser* 16 December 1922, 9 June 1923 and 28 September 1934.
26 *Ludlow Advertiser* 4 August 1900; 26 September 1947 & 17 November 1949.
27 *Ludlow Advertiser* 11 February 1922; 9 February 1924; 10 January 1925; 28 April 1928; 6 August 1929; 28 May 1932 and 27 April 1934.
28 Margery Spring Rice, *Working Class Wives* (First published London, 1939 and reprinted London, 1981).
29 Service Records viewed at Ancestry.com.
30 Ivan Hall, 'Out Relief in the 19th Century Ludlow Union' in *Victorian Ludlow* edited by Ludlow Historical Research Group (Bucknell, 2004).
31 Ludlow Charity Records 1869-72 and 1875-89 and annual Trade Directories (Ludlow Library Local History Collection.)
32 *Ibid.*
33 Various Trade Directories held in Ludlow Local Library and *Ludlow Advertiser* 9 February 1895, 26 November 1932 and 9 November 1934.
34 *Ludlow Advertiser* 7 December 1934 and 26 November 1932.
35 *Ludlow Advertiser* 16 and 23 February 1934 and 1 March 1946.
36 Derek Williams, *The Story of Ludlow Workhouse* (Logaston Press, 2012).
37 *Ludlow Advertiser* 10 February 1949.
38 *Ludlow Advertiser* 24 November 1949.

CHAPTER SIX

1   *Ludlow Advertiser* 23 February 1895.
2   *Hereford Journal* 8 December 1866.
3   *Ludlow Advertiser* 6 March 1909.
4   *Ludlow Advertiser* 14 February 1947.
5   *Ludlow Advertiser* 17 April and 26 November 1921.
6   *Ludlow Advertiser* 9 February 1929, 14 May 1932 and 21 January 1933.
7   *Hereford Journal* 31 January 1855.
8   A.E. Johnson, Primary and Secondary Education in Ludlow in the 19th Century (Unpublished dissertation, 1970) in Ludlow Library Local History Collection, *Shropshire Chronicle* 7 January 1870, *Ludlow Advertiser* 13 January 1894 and 23 February 1895.
9   *Ludlow Advertiser* 8 March 1924, 2 March 1929, 2 January 1932 and 11 and 25 February 1933.
10 *Ludlow Advertiser* 26 November 1921, 7 January 1922, 3 February 1923 and 14 January 1928.
11 *Ludlow Advertiser* 17 January 1885, 23 February 1895, 4 February 1899 and 5 January 1929.
12 *Ludlow Advertiser* 29 December 1933, 28 December 1934 and 3 January 1936.
13 *Ludlow Advertiser* 18 January 1946.
14 *Hereford Journal* 10 January 1850, *Ludlow Advertiser* 19 January 1895, 3 June 1922, 5 January 1924, 7 February 1925, 4 March 1933 and 16 March 1934.
15 *Ludlow Advertiser* 25 February 1933.
16 Poor Law Records for January 1886 in notes of Jean Brown, Ludlow Historical Research Group.
17 *Ludlow Advertiser* 6 May 1922.
18 Ludlow Charity Records 1869-72 and 1875-89 in Ludlow Library Local History Collection.
19 Martin Pugh, *We Danced All Night: A Social History of Britain Between the Wars* (London, 2008) pp. 233-34.
20 *Wellington Journal* 18 August 1866, and Police Charge Books 1865-72 and 1872-82 in Ludlow Museum Resource Centre.
21 A brothel was defined as a property where at least two prostitutes lived and carried on their trade. In Ludlow they tended to be run by a mature brothel keeper, usually a woman, with two or three prostitutes residing with her. The majority tended to be concentrated in Galdeford.
22 *Ludlow Advertiser* 8 June 1895.
23 A.E. Johnson 'Primary and Secondary Education in Ludlow' *op.cit.*
24 Police Charge Books *op.cit.* (Ludlow Museum and Resource Centre).
25 *Ludlow Advertiser* 22 October 1932.

26 *Ludlow Advertiser* 3 September 1932.
27 *Ludlow Advertiser* 21 August 1933.
28 *Ludlow Advertiser* 15 May 1920 and 17 February 1931.

CHAPTER SEVEN

1 All information for the working of the Addison Housing Act came from Derek Beattie, 'The origins, implementation and legacy of the Addison Housing Act 1919.' PhD thesis, Lancaster University 1986.
2 *Ludlow Advertiser* 5 July 1919, 16 August 1919 and 19 February 1920.
3 *Ludlow Advertiser* 9 February 1924.
4 *Ludlow Advertiser* 15 August 1925 and 9 and 17 January 1926.
5 *Ludlow Advertiser* 9 February 1929, 6 July 1929 and 28 September 1929.
6 *Ludlow Advertiser* 3 August 1929.
7 *Ludlow Advertiser* 3 May 1930.
8 *Ludlow Advertiser* 7 March 1931,13 February 1932, 5 March 1932 and 4 August 1933.
9 *Ludlow Advertiser* 9 April 1937, 14 January 1938 and Ludlow Council Housing and Estates Committee Minutes 16 May 1939 in author's possession.
10 All following details of post-war housing are taken from Ludlow Housing and Estate Committee Minutes 1928-1967 in author's possession.
11 *Ludlow Advertiser* 21 February 1947.
12 *Ludlow Heritage News* No 41 Winter 2004/5 and Housing and Estate Committee Minutes *op.cit.* 7 January and 3 November 1958.
13 Letter from Town Clerk to Society for the Protection of Historic Buildings dated 18 January 1958 in archives of that Society at 37, Spital Square, London E1.
14 *Daily Telegraph* 1 June 1959.
15 Letters to Town Clerk dated 1 May and 6 July 1959 in archives of Society for the Protection of Historic Buildings *op.cit.*
16 Letter from Kenneth Reid to the Society for the Protection of Historic Buildings dated 21 January 1969 in Societies archives *op.cit.*
17 All that follows on choice of tenants taken from Housing and Estate Committee Minutes *op.cit.* unless otherwise stated.
18 *Ludlow Advertiser* 5 October 1929, 15 February and 9 August 1930.
19 All that follows on modernization of council houses comes from Housing and Estate Committee Miutes *op.cit.* unless otherwise stated.
20 All that follows on housing situation 1955-1960 comes from Housing and Estate Committee Minutes *op.cit.* unless otherwise stated.

Interviewees

BURMINGHAM, DON – Born 1935 – father a platelayer on the railway and mother a part-time cleaner. One of seven children, six of who survived and childhood spent at 44, Old Street (corner of Old Street and Brand Lane) before moving to 18, Rock Lane on marriage in 1956. Then took over tenancy of mother-in-law's council house at 94, Sandpits Avenue.

BURMINGHAM, SHEILA née POSTANS - born 1937 at 48, Dinham but moved to council house at 94, Sandpits Avenue in 1939. Father a dustman before becoming a labourer on the railway. Mother worked at the laundry. On marriage in 1956, Sheila lived at 18, Rock Lane before taking her mother's tenancy back on Sandpits Avenue.

CLARE, ANGELA (ANGIE) née SWINDELLS – Born 1952. Father a labourer for Shropshire County Council. One of four sisters, Angie lived at the bottom of the Central Hall Yard off Upper Galdeford (formerly Page's Yard) before moving to a council house on the Dodmore Estate.

COX, GEORGE – Born 1935 - His father was a regular soldier who, after the war, joined the building trade. His mother was initially in service. George was one of five children and was born at 8, Raven Lane. The family lived there until moving to a council house on the Dodmore Estate c1950.

DONNELLY, ANN née JARVIS – Born 1939. Came to Ludlow from London as a teacher in 1960 and lived in 'digs' on Gravel Hill until 1963 when she moved to St John's Cottage on St John's Lane.

FRENCH, DAPHNE – Her father, one of eight children, was born in 1919 at 47, Whitcliffe Terrace off Lower Broad Street.

GRIFFITHS, JOSEPH – Born 1943. His father was a general labourer and his mother a member of a former travelling family. Joseph spent his early childhood at 42, Old Street until moving to a council house on Sandpits Avenue. He was the youngest of eight children.

GRIFFITHS, JOSEPH (JOE) – Born 1931 - His father was a timber loader with the railway company. One of seven children, Joe lived at 41, Upper Galdeford (Page's Yard – later known as the Central Hall Yard). He left in 1951 to live in his first marital home at 10, Rock Lane.

HOWARD, WINIFRED née FELTON – Born 1936. Lived with her mother, stepfather and eight siblings. Her mother worked as cleaner and washerwoman at some of the larger houses in town. Winifred's early life was spent at 120, Old Street until the family moved to a council house in Sandpits Avenue.

JONES, EILEEN née MATTHEWS – Born 1947 at 13, St John's Road. Eileen was one of five children, four of whom survived.

JONES, ROBERT (BOB) – Born 1954 in St Stephen's Yard off Upper Galdeford. Bob was one of eight children and his father was a slaughterman.

JONES, SUSAN (SUE) née REECE – Born in Haytons Bent in 1950. After her father left home in 1953 she came with her mother and two elder sisters to live at 14, Rock Lane. Her mother worked as a cleaner at Marston's Offices on Corve Street before working for butchers on the Bull Ring (now Griffiths). In 1961 the family moved to a council house at 58, Sandpits Avenue.

LEWIS, DOREEN née HONEY – Born 1931. One of six children, Doreen was evacuated from Plaistow, East London in 1939 and reunited with her mother in Ludlow in 1944. In 1945 Doreen, together with her mother and four siblings shared 14, Broad Street with another family. After marriage Doreen lived with her husband's family before moving to 53, Lower Broad Street in the mid 1950s with her husband and two children. Two more children then followed.

McGARRITY, MARGARET – Born 1937. Her father was related to a travelling family and was employed as a drover pre-1939. After the war he became a general labourer on the railway before joining the Midland Electricity Company. Margaret was the second eldest of six children and lived at 7, Taylor's Court off Lower Broad Street until 1952 when the family moved to a council house on the Dodmore estate.

MARSH, JOHN – Born 1933. His father was a builder's labourer. John was one of three children. He was born at 7, Lower Mill Street though the family moved next door to No 8 when he was still a young child. John left home when he married in 1959.

MATTHEWS, THOMAS (RUSTY) – Born 1945. Father was a dustman. Rusty was one of five children, four of whom survived childhood. The family lived at 13, St John's Road.

NEWMAN, MICHAEL – Born 1937 in Halford's Yard off Raven Lane. His father was a confectioner at De Greys before serving in the Royal Navy during the war. On his return he became a general labourer in the building trade. His mother took in washing. Michael was the second eldest of seven children. In 1947 the family moved to a flat in Springfield House off Lower Galdeford before moving again into a council house on Sandpits Avenue in 1959.

OLIVER, BRENDA née MASSAM – Born 1939. Her father was a groom before starting work as a railway labourer. Brenda was the middle child of three. The family lived at 85 (Lower) Corve Street until moving to a council house on the Dodmore estate c1948.

PARKER, JEAN née EDWARDS – Born 1956. Her father was a farmworker. The family lived at 35, Steventon New Road until 1970.

POUND, ALICE née SWINDELLS – Born 1944. Father was a labourer for Shropshire County Council. Alice lived with her three sisters at the bottom of the Central Hall Yard off Upper Galdeford (formerly Page's Yard) before moving to a council house on the Dodmore estate.

ROBERTSON, QUILLER née NORTHWOOD – Born 1944. Father was a carpenter. Quiller was one of three children and lived at 7, Warrington Gardens. Her maternal grandmother brought up her family at 18, Linney and still lived there in the 1950s when Quiller often stayed with her.

SADLER, PHILLIP – Born 1944. His father was a baker and later a driver for the Midland Red Bus Company. His mother was a packer for Gaius Smith, Grocers before becoming a homeworker making boxes. Phillip was the eldest of three children. When he was a young child his parents lived with his maternal grandmother at 21, New Street before moving to a new council house property at 41, Clee View in 1949.

SAMPSON, ELFREDA née COMPTON – Born 1923. Elfreda came to Ludlow in 1942 after her marriage to a GPO engineer. Elfreda worked as a GPO telephonist. Their first home was at 33, New Road and they had two children.

STEPHENS, SHEILA née MADDOX – Born 1937. Her father was a boot and shoe repairer who had a workshop in his garden. Sheila was one of three children and, as a baby, moved to 35, Lower Broad Street where she lived until her marriage in 1956.

STEWART, FREDA née LOCKETT – Born 1929. Father a labourer on the railway. One of ten children nine of whom survived childhood. Freda lived with her parents at 3, Holdgate Fee (at the entrance to Grieve's Yard and later renumbered as 95 Old Street) before moving to a council house at 101, Sandpits Avenue c1940. Though married in 1956, Freda remained at her parents' house until moving with her husband to a new home in the 1960s.

TAYLOR, JEAN née GRAHAM – Born 1954. Father worked at McConnells. Jean was an only child and was born at 66 Holdgate Fee (opposite the Hen and Chickens public house). In c1960 the family moved to 67, Upper Galdeford.

THOMAS, JOAN née POUND – Born 1928. Father was a labourer for the Birmingham Water Company. Joan was one of seven children of whom five survived – three boys and two girls. All were born at 80, Lower Galdeford before the family moved in 1937 to a council house at 38, Sandpits Avenue. On marriage in the 1950s, Joan moved to 31, Rock Lane.

WEAVER, DAVID – Born 1933. His father was a baker's roundsman whilst his mother worked as a cleaner at weekends. He was the younger of two brothers and lived at 6, Portcullis Lane until his marriage in 1955.

WEAVER, MARILYN – Born 1936. One of two children, her father was a smallholder and dealer in cattle. He also worked for various auctioneers. Her mother ran a sweet shop at 2, Market Street above and behind which the family lived. On marriage in 1957 Marilyn moved to a flat above a butchers shop at 1, Market Street.

Index

Bell Lane	*132*	Whitbread Road	158
Belle Vue Terrace (*see* Chapel Row)		Courts and Yards	
Brand Lane	36	Badger's Yard	6, 97-98
Brickyard	37, 49-50, 55, 77	Breakell's Yard	5
Broad Street	8, 44, *52*, 68, 110, *118*, 124, 129, 152	Burnsnell's Yard	6
		Central Hall Yard	5, 13, 37, 50, *65*, 78, 80, 130
Bull Ring	4, 44, *48*, 55, *89*, 138, *144*	Chapel Yard	6, *47*
Buttercross	117, *121*	Davies' Yard	6, 25
Castle Square	42, 139	Dean's Yard	6, 7, 27, 31
Castle Street	110	Drew's Court/Yard	*3*, 4, 26
Chapel Row (Belle Vue Terrace)	47, 55, 86	Green Dragon Yard	4, *72*
Church Street	123	Grey's Yard	6
Clothing	127-29	Greyhound Yard	5, 27, 37, *44*, 52
College Street	*28*, 88, *90*, 111	Grieves' Yard	6, 50
Corve Street	3-5, 9, 14-15, 16, 21, *24*, 25, 30, 35, 45, 50, *51*, 60, *71*, *72*, 77, 81, *85*, 85, 92, *95*, *97*, 97, *99*, 105, 128, 136, *137*, 143, 144, *146*, 160, 161, 164, *167*	Halford's Yard	14
		Hammond's Court	3
		Hartland's Yard	8
		Hince's Yard	6
		Jones' Yard (Lower G)	6
Council Housing	70-71, 77, 148-58	Jones' Yard (Upper G)	5, 25
Amenities	164-70	King's Arms Yard	*4*, 29
Clee View	157	Martha Cad's Yard	6
Dodmore Estate	13, *151*, 156-57, 166-67	Maund's Yard	8, *69*, 72-73
		Nag's Head Yard	4, 26, *95*
Henley Road	152, 165	Noakes Yard	6, 7, *126*
Jack's Meadow Scheme	156, 169	Old Chapel Yard	5
Riddings Road	157	Page's Yard	5, 31, 55, *65*
Sandpits Avenue	100, 132, 155, 163, 165-66	Pardoe's Yard	6, 9, 29
		Pearce's Court	5
Sandpits Lane	*149*, 152	Preece's Court	5
Sandpits Road	158, 165	Price's Yard	5
Steventon Crescent	62, 153-54, 157, *158*, 165, 166	Roger's Yard	26
		Sheldon's Yard	5, 27, 31
Steventon Road	157, 158	Shenton's Yard	5
Temeside Estate	149-51, 164-5	Sims Yard	8
Tenants	162-64, *165*	St Stephen's Yard	5, 12, 50
Wheeler Road	157		

Three Horseshoes Yard 5
Tallowfat Yard 6
Taylor's Court 8, 12, 29, 50, 55, 69, 78, 166
Tin Yard 5
Vineyard 8, *37*
Warrington's Yard 5
Watkin's Yard 6, 27
Weaver's Yard 6, 50
Whitcliffe Terrace 8, 55
Credit 133-34
Dinham 2, 8, 105, *131*
Disease
  Diptheria 88-90
  Scarlet Fever 88, 89
  Smallpox 86-88
  Tuberculosis 88, 91-94
  Typhoid 45, 47-49, 85-86
Dodmore Lane 47, 77
Drainage 27-30, *30*
East Hamlet 35, 47, *145*
Food 130-33, *135, 160*
Frog Lane (*see* St John's Road)
Galdeford (*see* Upper and Lower Galdeford)
Gravel Hill 19, 35, 46, 113, *153*
Harp Lane *92*
Health/Healthcare 110-115
  Children 10, 87, 88
  Housewives 106-08
  Infants 98-108
  Men 109
Henley Road 127
High Street 128
Holdgate Fee 6, 13, 16, 20, 25, 39, 44, 50, 51, 60, *66, 76,* 76-77, 78, 80, 87, 99, 129, *157, 165*
Holidays 134-36

Hospitals
  Cottage 88, *90,* 111-12, 113, 114
  East Hamlet 114
  Isolation (First) 87
  Isolation (Second) 90-91
  Workhouse Infirmary *103*, 113-14
Illegitimacy 101-02
Lighting 80-83, *153*, 166-67
Linney 20, 34, 37, 39, 44, 73-74, 92
Lodgers/Lodging Houses 14-18, 87
Lower Broad Street 7-8, 11, 12, 13-14, 15, 16, 27, 29, *30, 37*, 43, 50, 55, 56, 57, 59, *67*, 69, 77, 78, 80, 83, 98, 99, 112, *129, 140*, 144, 159, 166
Lower Galdeford 5-6, 11, 14, 15, 16, *18*, 35, 41, 49, 55, 59, 60, 61, 69, 71, 73, 77, 81, *81, 82*, 82, 83, 98, 116, 120, 121, 123, 136, 137-8, 139, 166
Lower Mill Street 13, 31, 42, 45, 46, 55, 56, *58*, 77, 80, 83, 101, *150*, 160-61
Ludford *34*, 49
Market Street 57, *122*, 134
Markets and Fairs 138-39, *143*
Mill Street 8, *69*, 72-73, *75*, 77, 139, 159-60
New Road *31*, 47, 49, 53, 102
New Street *33, 42*, 47, 54, *151*
Old Street 6, 7, 9, 12, 13, *15*, 16, 20, 26, 27, 31, 32, 37, *47*, 50, 56, 58, 60, 62. 77, 79, 81, 92, 123, 129, 130, 132, *138, 139, 147*, 156
Overcrowding 10-15
Part-time work *125*, 139-46
Pedlars and Hawkers *8*, 19-20
Pepper Lane 82
Portcullis Lane 39, 49, 51, 52, 80, *153*
Privies/Water Closets 23-27, *27*, 30-34, *32*, 35-40

Index

Prostitution 136-39
Pynfold Close 5
Quality Square 92, 94, 96, 98, *107*
Raven Lane 8, 13, 14, *27*, 37, 50, 60, 80, 105, 136
Renovation of Houses *150*, 159-61, *167*
Rock Lane 50, 51, 52, 77, 78, 80, 81, 87, 89, 125
Sandpits 77, 146
Sewerage 23, 34-35
Silk Mill Lane 50, 136
Slaughterhouses *92*, 94-98
Smithfield 34, 87, 124, 138, 156
Soup Kitchens/poor relief 119-126, *144*, 147
St John's Lane 20, 60, 77, 78, *79*, 136, *154*, 155, 156, *163*
St John's Road 6, 14, *15*, 20, 26, 27, 28, *37*, 37, 43, *53*, 60, *66*, 77, 105, 126, 129, 156
St Mary's Lane 11, 25, 50, *70*, 77, 92, *100*, 168

Steventon New Road 48
Steventon Road 39
Temeside 34, 35, 44
Tower Street 4, 6, 29, 50, 60, *96*, *138*
Trades and Industries 1, *9, 10, 17,* 20-22, *145*
Unemployment 22, 116-19, *121*, 124-26
Upper Galdeford 5, 12, 13, 16, *21*, 27, 31, 32, 36, 37, 50, 52, 55, 60, 62, 77, 78, 80, *82*, 82, 130, 136
Vermin 78-80
Warrington Gardens 5
Wash Houses/Laundry *27, 42, 52,* 53-60, *54, 56*
Washing – Personal *45*, 60-63
Water Supply 41-53, *43, 58*, 164-65, 167-68
Waterside 16-18
Workhouse *12*, 19, *20*, 46, 87, *103*
Yards (*see* Courts and Yards)

Green Dragon Yard, Lower Corve Street. 1962

Acknowledgements

In addition to the kind people who related their early life experiences to me I need to especially thank the staff at the Ludlow Museum and Resource Centre who have now sadly been made redundant. My thanks must also be given to the staff at the Shropshire Archives and Ludlow Library who helped in such a professional manner. Roy Payne, a fellow member of the Ludlow Historical Research Group, requires a special mention for reading my first draft with such meticulous care. Lottie and Debbie James have generously allowed me to reproduce the photos on pages i, 3, 38 and 95 from the photo album created by their great aunt, Jane Green. Finally, I must thank Merlin, Karen and Jo at Merlin Unwin Books for their kind patience and help.

Chipps Furniture Shop, Ludlow

Also published by Merlin Unwin Books

Myddle *The Life and Times of a Shropshire Farmworker's Daughter* Helen Ebrey £12

Temptation & Downfall of the Vicar of Stanton Lacy Peter Klein £12

It Happened in Shropshire Bob Burrows £8.99

A View from the Tractor Roger Evans £12

A Farmer's Lot Roger Evans £12

Over the Farmer's Gate Roger Evans £6.75 ebook

Much Ado About Mutton Bob Kennard £20

A Most Rare Vision *Shropshire from the Air* Mark Sisson £14.99

Extraordinary Villages Tony Francis £14.99

The Byerley Turk *The True Story of the First Thoroughbred* Jeremy James £8.99 pb / £6.75 ebook

Maynard: *The Adventures of a Bacon Curer* Maynard Davies £9.99 hb / £5.99 ebk

Maynard: *The Secrets of a Bacon Curer* Maynard Davies £9.99 hb / £5.99 ebk

Recollections of a Moorland Lad Richard Robinson £12

Living off the Land Frances Mountford £12.99

Available from all good bookshops
Full details of all our books: www.merlinunwin.co.uk

May 25